MICROSOFT
WORD®
MADE EASY

ROB HAWKINS

**FLAME TREE
PUBLISHING**

CONTENTS

New to Word? Need to brush up on your word processing skills? This chapter includes a comprehensive list of word processor jargon and examples of how the program can be used. There's an illustrative guide to what's on the Word screen for most versions of the program and no-nonsense instructions on the best ways of getting started, including opening files, saving work, finding files and moving around a document.

CREATING A DOCUMENT..................... 54

Word is a relatively simple program to start using, but there are right and wrong ways to use it. This chapter shows the best-practice methods for using the program to create a document, explaining the quickest ways to type, select, copy and move text. There are also clear details on changing the view of a document and printing it.

IMPROVING A DOCUMENT 88

A document can always be improved upon and this chapter shows all the shortcuts and effective ways of making your work look professional and impressive. There's information on using headings, styles and themes, organizing text with lists and tables, using images and adding colour. Professional-looking additions, including charts and diagrams, are examined, with information on how to include them in a document such as a report.

TIME SAVERS & TROUBLESHOOTING 120

There are lots of quicker and faster ways of using Word, so this chapter has picked out the popular time savers, including how Word automatically corrects mistakes and inserts text for you. There's information on identifying where a document has been changed and understanding the structure of complex documents. The end of the chapter outlines many of the typical problems experienced with Word and how to resolve them.

CREATING PROFESSIONAL DOCUMENTS .. 156

This chapter is the most practical and covers creating a wide range of documents with many step-by-step guides providing clear and easy-to-follow instructions. Pick any section within this chapter and you don't need to have read anything else in the book to complete it. If you want to write a book, or produce a poster, CV or questionnaire, you'll find out how in this chapter.

ADVANCED WORD

Ever wondered what a macro is or how mail merge works in Word? This chapter has all the answers to such queries and more. Whether you want to include a calculation in a document, understand how tabs work, create a table of authorities for a legal document or protect a document, all of these subjects are covered. There's also clear and concise information on specific tasks, including printing on to envelopes and labels, plus more generic but just as labour-saving tasks, including using voice recognition to dictate typing.

INTRODUCTION

Since Microsoft Word first appeared nearly three decades ago, this computerized typewriter has gradually become a market leader. It has evolved over the years with an increasing number of features that can be confusing to beginners and more experienced users alike. This book aims to cut through that confusion and provide a practical education in the use of Word and how it can be used correctly and efficiently.

WORD HAS EVOLVED

Word can be used for a wide range of purposes. Traditionally, it was used for typing correspondence and reports, so it was initially designed around the purposes of a typewriter. However, it has become more sophisticated and many people have realized the benefit of using it to produce training manuals, leaflets, posters, web pages and books. At home, there are plenty of uses, including writing an annual Christmas letter or producing a wedding invitation and using mail merge to save time writing individual addresses. If you need to produce a notice or leaflet, Word can quickly produce a colourful document that looks professional.

NEED TO KNOW

Whilst the ideas for using Word can keep on growing, the problem with such a program is understanding how to use it and making sure that whatever is created is correct. Creating a macro or an AutoText entry to save time in the future takes some planning and requires an understanding of how these tools are used. This book provides the guidance and practical advice to help resolve such dilemmas. Whilst most people find Word an easy program to use to type a letter for instance, the more complicated features need accurate information and help. Also, it's essential to have an understanding of the jargon and terminology used by Word to avoid moments of frustration and confusion, so we've defined lots of Word and word processor jargon.

Above: There is a vast assortment of pre-created documents in Word, which can help save time with producing professional-looking material.

DIFFERENCES

One particularly frustrating point concerning Word is its differences between the versions of the program. The program has been updated and changed more than a dozen times since it was first introduced nearly 30 years ago. In 2007, Microsoft made some extensive alterations to the look of Word, some of which divided opinion. This book can be applied to most of the versions of Word, but many of the instructions and details relate to Word 97, 2000, 2002, 2003, 2007 and 2010. Where appropriate, instructions and information state to which versions of Word they apply.

SMALL CHUNKS

There is one theme that has been carried through this book. Flick through the pages and there are always short paragraphs describing particular features within Word and how to use them. Upon first sight, it may look like the text of this book has to be read in order, but all of the sections are task-oriented, so they can be read and practised individually. Pick out the section on writing a report for example, and it can be read and used on its own.

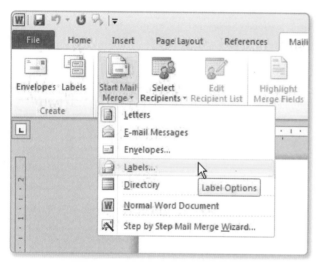

Above: Word's automated features save time printing on to labels and envelopes, and producing mail merged letters and emails.

STEP-BY-STEP

Throughout the book there are step-by-step guides covering everything from creating a CV, invitation or a leaflet, to planning a holiday, writing a book or producing a dissertation. Each step-by-step guide explains which menus or buttons to click on and what to expect when you follow the instructions. Any differences between the various versions of Word are explained, so you can be confident the step-by-step information can be applied to your version of the program. Difficult topics, including macros, mail merge, inserting an index, creating endnotes and writing formulas, are all covered in clear and concise steps.

HELP!

If you're stuck on a particular topic, please email Flame Tree Publishing at support@flametreepublishing.com. While we cannot operate a 24-hour helpline for all your Word needs, we will answer your query via email.

TRAINING AND CONSULTANCY

The contents of this book have been researched through a decade and a half of delivering Word training courses using versions as early as 6.0 and as up to date as 2010. The author, Rob Hawkins, has taught hundreds of people to use Word at a variety of levels, ranging from absolute beginners to advanced users and from typists to company directors.

RESEARCH FINDINGS

The findings from the author's training and consultancy concerning Word are now very different to 15 years ago, when many people were struggling to use a mouse and recognize buttons on the screen for saving, opening and closing files. Nowadays, most people have a better skill level, but there are still a few gaps, which we've tried to outline in this book.

Above: Images can be inserted into a document. Word has a large library of Clip Art and photographs that can be used.

Many people struggle with understanding tabs and applying heading levels, and most people have heard of macros but don't know what they are. All of this and more is outlined clearly and concisely in this book. There are also many shortcuts that most people are not aware of, which can save hours of time, so the most popular and useful of these have been outlined.

SIX CHAPTERS

In brief, the contents of this book are split into six chapters, which begin with some probing questions about the use of Word, what it is and what all the jargon means. The second chapter covers the quick techniques for creating a document, selecting text, copying and moving text, changing the view and printing. Chapter three is useful for anyone wanting to improve a document with headings, tables, bulleted lists, images and colours. Chapter four aims to outline all the quick techniques for saving time when creating and editing a document, plus there are several pages covering typical problems found in Word and how to fix them. Chapter five is purely task-specific and is for anyone wanting to use Word to carry out such jobs as writing a book or dissertation, designing a poster, producing a CV or creating a questionnaire. Finally, chapter six covers many of the advanced topics found in Word and provides clear descriptions and instructions on how to use them, ranging from mail merge and macros to creating an index and using speech recognition.

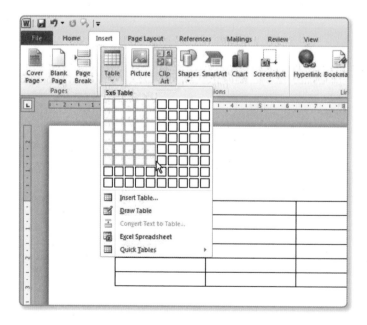

Left: A wide range of objects can be added to a document, including tables, charts and clip art.

HOT TIPS AND SHORTCUTS

Within each section of this book, look out for the Hot Tips, which provide useful hints associated with the topic being covered. There are many shortcuts and quick techniques available in Word and we've tried to highlight many of them through these easy-to-spot Hot Tips. They can often be spotted by flicking through the pages of the book and, in many cases, you don't need to read through the section they're in to understand and use them.

UNDERSTAND MORE, ACHIEVE MORE

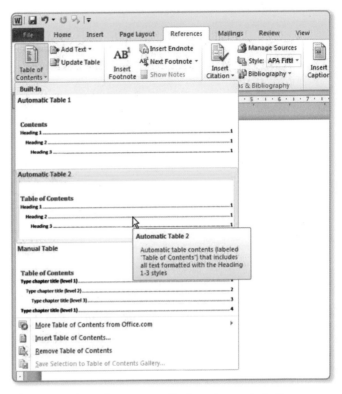

Above: Large reports, dissertations and books can be organized with a contents table that is quick and easy to insert into a Word document

Microsoft Word can shave hours off a working week with automatic corrections, templates and other pre-made documents, but if you're armed with insufficient or incorrect knowledge, it can become a living nightmare, resulting in hours of wasted time, frustration and poorly presented documents. *Microsoft Word Made Easy* has been written with the intention of using Word more efficiently and producing more professional-looking documents. Every page tries to educate the reader, save time when producing documents and help improve the presentation of work produced in Microsoft Word. Whether you are a novice with Word or know the contents of every menu, this book provides the information and guidance to cover both ends of the experience spectrum. Using this book will show you how useful Word really can be.

WORD GROUND RULES

WHAT IS A WORD PROCESSOR?

A word processor is the computer equivalent of a typewriter, but with many more features that can save time and reduce mistakes. The following pages outline how the word processor has evolved and the history of Microsoft Word.

WORD PROCESSOR EVOLUTION

The word processor was designed along the lines of the typewriter and evolved accordingly. Early versions used typewriter features, still available today, including tabs and line spacing. Consequently, the early word processor programs required some knowledge of using a typewriter to be able to understand the terminology.

Other Word Processors

Some of the popular word processor programs that appeared in the Eighties included Wordstar, WordPerfect, Write and Mac Write. WordPerfect became a market leader during the Eighties, but Microsoft Word slowly started to become the dominant force during the late Nineties and eventually took the lead in the first decade of the twenty-first century.

Free Word Processors

There are a number of free word processors, similar to Microsoft Word. Here are some of them:

- **Open Office:** This is an office suite of free-to-use programs, including a word processor, spreadsheet and presentation program. Visit www.openoffice.org to download the software.

- **AbiWord:** A free word processor that is similar to Microsoft Word. First released in October 2009 and available to download for free from www.abisource.com.

Jarte: Based on Microsoft's WordPad and available to download for free from www.jarte.com.

WordPad: Available for free with Microsoft Windows. A simplistic but useful word processor.

WYSIWYG

One of the most essential developments in word processing was to ensure that the layout and the style of the words on the screen would look exactly the same when printed. This is known as WYSIWYG, which stands for What You See Is What You Get. Nowadays, we take this for granted, but during the Eighties, many word processors could not offer this feature.

Left: Free word processors such as Jarte share many features similar to Microsoft Word.

WORD VERSIONS

The origins of Microsoft Word can be traced back to 1983 when it was called Multi-Tool Word and was first available for Xenix computer systems, followed by PCs using MS-DOS. It was initially launched as a free program to *PC World* magazine subscribers and available on a floppy diskette. The program was developed for the Apple Macintosh in 1984 and other computers over the following years.

Hot Tip

Which version have I got? Click on the Help menu and select About Microsoft Office Word. A box will appear displaying the version of Word at the top. If you can't see a Help menu, click on the question mark at the top-right corner of the screen. A separate box will appear, displaying the version of Word you are using.

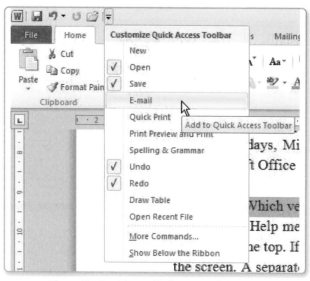

Above: The Quick Access Toolbar is one of the many new features found in Word 2007 and 2010.

Nowadays, Microsoft Word is mostly used on the PC and Apple Mac and is available as part of the Microsoft Office Suite or in a simpler form as part of Microsoft Works.

Upgrading to Word 2007 and 2010

If you've been using Word 2003 or a previous version for several years, then Word 2007 or 2010 will seem very different in comparison. These later versions of the program use ribbon tabs and buttons instead of a menu bar and toolbar buttons. However, the ribbon tabs (Home, Insert, Page Layout, View) are similar in some cases to the older versions of Word and the ribbon buttons that appear after clicking on a ribbon tab are also familiar. Here are some of the main differences that can cause confusion:

- **Office button (Word 2007 only):** There is no File ribbon tab in Word 2007, but instead there is a multi-coloured Office button in the top-left corner of the screen. Click on this to see a similar list of options to the traditional File menu.

- **Quick Access Toolbar:** There are some traditional toolbar buttons in the top-left corner of the screen, which are located on the Quick Access Toolbar. More buttons can be added here.

- **Missing menu options and buttons:** If a specific feature is missing in Word 2007–2010, it may have to be added to the Quick Access Toolbar. Click on the button to the right of the Quick Access Toolbar and choose any of the listed buttons to add them, or select More Commands to find other features to add.

Interactive ribbon tabs: When a table or chart is inserted, or a similar additional feature, new ribbon tabs appear with additional ribbon buttons to enable that object or feature to be edited.

Shortcut buttons: If some text is selected, a small block of toolbar buttons appears when the mouse pointer is positioned over the selected text. These buttons allow the formatting of the selected text to be changed. They also appear upon right clicking inside a document or selected text.

Word on the Macintosh

Although the Apple Macintosh computer has its own operating system, Microsoft has developed Word to work in much the same way as it does on a Windows platform. Word for Windows and Word for the Mac share a common interface and functionality, making it easier for companies to support both platforms, and file compatibility between the two operating systems is very high, enabling users to share files between PCs and Macs. This book has been written for all versions of Word for the PC, but most of the information can be applied to the Apple Mac. See pages 35–36 to see the similarities and differences on screen between the PC and the Mac, and for a note on keyboards.

WORD VERSIONS AND YEARS (PC AND MAC)

Year	Computer type	Comments
1983	Xenix and PC with MS-DOS	Word 1.0 available for free to *PC World* magazine subscribers
1984	Apple Mac	First version of Word for the Apple Mac

1986	Atari ST	Word 1.05
1987	Apple Mac	Word 3.0 followed by 3.0.1
1989	PC with Windows	First version of Word for Windows
1991	PC with MS-DOS	Word 5.5 for MS-DOS
1992	PC with Windows or MS-DOS and Apple Mac	Word 6.0
1995	PC with Windows	Word 95 (part of Office 95)
1997	PC with Windows	Word 97 (part of Office 97)
1998	Apple Mac	Word 98
2000	Apple Mac	Word 2001
2000	PC with Windows	Word 2000 (part of Office 2000)
2002	PC with Windows	Word 2002 (part of Office XP)
2003	PC with Windows	Word 2003 (part of Office XP)
2004	Apple Mac	Word 2004
2007	PC with Windows	Word 2007 (parts of Office 2007)
2008	Apple Mac	Word 2008
2010	PC with Windows	Word 2010 (part of Office 2010)
2010	Apple Mac	Word 2011

WORD JARGON

Word processor programs have a vast assortment of technical terms, which can be confusing and misleading if you don't know what they mean. AutoText, heading levels and section breaks are useful tools in Word, but only if you know what they are and how to use them. The following section lists and defines some of the commonly used word processor terminology.

AUTOCORRECT

Word can automatically correct spelling mistakes. This is called AutoCorrect and is covered in more depth in chapter four.

AUTOTEXT

This is text that can be instantly entered into a document without having to type all of it. It saves time on typing and is useful for text ranging from a few words to whole paragraphs.

BOOKMARK

Specific points in a document can be labelled as bookmarks. This makes it quicker to find places in a document.

DOCUMENT

A document in Word is a file containing one or more pages. The document is saved with a filename, followed by the extension .doc in Word pre-2007, or .docx in Word 2007 and later versions.

FOOTNOTE

Non-fiction books often use notes at the bottom of the page, which refer to particular points in the text. These are known as footnotes and can be created in Microsoft Word.

Above: Headings are found along the top of the screen on the Home ribbon tab in Word 2007 and later versions.

HEADINGS

Headings in Word can be used to label chapter headings, section headings and sub-headings. Word uses a numbered system for headings, starting at Heading 1, followed by Heading 2, Heading 3, and so on. This is useful for creating a hierarchical structure (Heading 1 could be a chapter heading, whereas Heading 3 might be a sub-heading). Each heading is known as a style. This is covered in more depth in chapter three.

MACRO

An automated procedure or sequence of procedures, which saves times having to do them yourself. For example, if a paragraph in a letter has to be displayed in Arial 12 with bold and underline, a macro can be created to apply this formatting. Macros can be played back by pressing pre-set keyboard keys (for example, Ctrl+Q) or by assigning them to toolbar buttons.

MAIL MERGE

Microsoft Word can print or email multiple copies of a document and insert personal details or other information into each copy. Whilst this is typical of what is commonly known as junk mail, this has its uses, including Christmas letters, invitations and change of address letters.

MARGINS

The space at the top, bottom, left and right of a page between the edge of the text and the edge of the page. The margins determine how close to the edge of a page the text is displayed and printed. The amount of space is measured in centimetres or inches and can be changed.

PAGE BREAK

When a new page is started in a document, this is technically known as a page break. A new page or page break starts when the text has filled the current page, or a page break can be purposely inserted.

RULER

A ruler can be displayed along the top of a page and down the left side. This helps to work out how much space has been used on a page and is especially useful for tables and columns of text.

Above: The Ruler is displayed along the top of the page and down the left side. It helps to show the size of margins and where text and images are positioned.

SECTION BREAK

If a document uses particular fonts, colours or page layouts (for example, landscape A4) in one part and different settings in another, these formatting and page set-up details can be separated with a section break.

STYLES

A style represents the details applied to text, such as the font type, size, colour and whether italic or bold is used. Pre-set styles include Normal for the main text in a document, Heading 1 and Heading 2 for a main heading and sub-heading, and Hyperlink for a website address. Using styles ensures the formatting is the same for particular types of text throughout a document. Pre-set styles are always available, but you can also make your own.

TABS

Pre-set spaces between text, useful for creating multiple lists on a page. Tabs are a traditional feature of typewriters, but have been replaced in many cases by tables, which are easier to use.

TEMPLATE

A pre-created document that can be reused without destroying the original. This is ideal for saving time on typing and can be used for letters, faxes and leaflets.

WHAT CAN I DO WITH WORD?

Microsoft Word's word processing capabilities are very sophisticated, but extremely useful. Here are a few examples of what you can create.

WRITE A BOOK

Word is capable of managing a document containing thousands or hundreds of thousands of words. It can display word counts, organize chapters with headings and sub-headings, create a contents and index, and automatically update footnotes. Whether a book is fact or fiction, Word can help with its creation.

BUSINESS REPORTS

Reports for work can often become complicated, with sales information from other sources, charts and accounting data. Word can store a vast assortment of information from other sources in a document. It also has features to create charts, add calendars, insert images and create tables to help further enhance a report.

UNIVERSITY DISSERTATION OR THESIS

Large and complicated assignments such as a 15,000-word dissertation can be created in Word and many of its time-saving features can be used. Footnotes, references, indexes and a contents page can all be created and automatically updated whenever changes are made or new text is added. Word counts are quick to display for the entire text or parts of the document, and when the completed masterpiece is ready to be professionally printed and bound, it can be emailed directly to a printer.

Right: Word can help create professional-looking posters and leaflets.

POSTERS AND LEAFLETS

Word isn't just useful for creating documents full of text. It can also be more creative and artistic, proving handy for notices. The program has a library of images (Clip Art), its own drawing tools and a wide range of fonts and colours to include in a poster, leaflet or flyer.

NEWSLETTERS

You don't need to learn the technicalities of desktop publishing with Word to be able to create a newsletter. Multiple columns, borders and images can all be created in a newsletter format using Word.

LETTERS

Your address, the current date and a signature can all be created and included in a letter that can be re-used and changed time and time again. Word can save hours of typing your address

and any frequently used paragraphs of text. Just type it once and it's saved for using again in the future.

SEND A FAX

Whether you have a fax machine or not, Word can be set up to fax a document created in the program. You can create your own fax from a blank document in Word, or there is a time-saving fax template.

CREATE A PDF

The Portable Document Format (PDF) is a popular type of file that can be shared around the world and opened by most computers. Microsoft Word 2007 and later versions can save a document as a PDF.

MAKE A WEB PAGE

A document created in Word can be saved as a web page and viewed using a web browser such as Internet Explorer, Google Chrome or Mozilla Firefox. If you are new to creating websites and would like to produce a web page, Word is a good starting point.

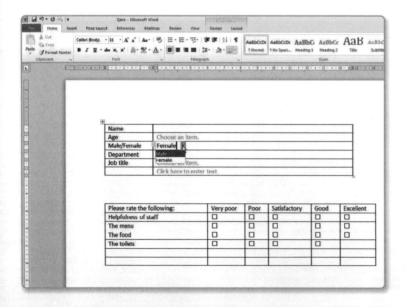

FILL IN A FORM

Save time at work by creating expenses claim forms, questionnaires and other official documents in Word. Columns of numbers can be totalled for adding up expenses and tick boxes can be included to choose options in questionnaires.

Left: Word's form tools are useful for creating questionnaires.

THE WORD WINDOW

The main screen in Word can seem bewildering if you don't know what you're looking for and don't recognize any of the symbols on it. The following pages provide detailed explanations of the various aspects of the Word screen, ranging from the older editions to the latest 2007–2010 versions.

WORD PRE-2007 ON THE PC

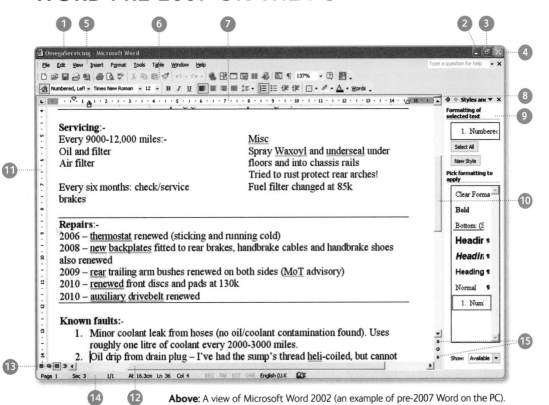

Above: A view of Microsoft Word 2002 (an example of pre-2007 Word on the PC).

1. **Title bar:** The title bar appears at the top of all Microsoft applications. It displays the name of the application and current document in the top-left corner.

2. **Minimize button:** Click on this button to hide the Word window and display whatever is behind it (another Word document if more are open). The document can be retrieved by clicking on its icon on the taskbar at the bottom of the screen.

3. **Maximize/Restore button:** If this button shows a single box, clicking on it will fill the Word page to the full size of the screen (maximize). If two boxes are shown (restore), clicking on it will reduce the Word screen so that other programs and the desktop can be seen.

4. **Close button:** Click on this to close the Word document that is displayed on screen. Depending on the version of Word, either the document on screen will be closed or Word and all documents that are open will be closed.

5. **Menu bar:** A series of drop-down menus, activated by clicking on the words across the top of the screen (File, Edit, View).

6. **Toolbar:** Word provides a full range of toolbars, each containing a number of toolbar buttons. These buttons provide a shortcut to commonly used features.

7. **Horizontal ruler:** Displays the horizontal dimensions (width) of the document in inches or centimetres. Click on the View menu and choose Ruler if it's not visible.

8. **Vertical split box:** This split box can be used to split or divide the window vertically so that you can view two areas of the worksheet at the same time. Drag the split box down the scroll bar to the position where you want the window split.

9. **Task pane (Word 2002–2003):** Displays some of the commonly used tasks in Word. Click on the View menu and choose Task Pane to switch it on or off.

10. **Vertical scroll bar**: The vertical scroll bar allows you to scroll up and down a document.

11. **Vertical ruler**: Displays the vertical dimensions (height) of each page in inches or centimetres.

12. **Horizontal scroll bar**: Only displayed when the entire width of a page is too wide to be displayed on the screen. Provides left and right scrolling across the document.

13. **Layouts**: Click on the small buttons to change to different views of the document, including Normal, Web Layout, Print Layout and Outline.

14. **Status bar**: The left side of the status bar displays the number of pages in the document and which page is on screen, plus the current position of the cursor. The middle of the status bar displays settings concerning track changes, over-typing (Insert key on the keyboard) and which language is used for checking spelling.

15. **Page up/down**: Scrolls up and down one page at a time.

WORD 2007-2010 ON THE PC

The screen for Word 2007 and 2010 looks very different to any previous versions of Word. However, there are several similarities, including scroll bars, minimize and maximize buttons, and rulers. New features include the replacement of the menu bar and toolbar buttons with a selection of ribbons. These are selected via a series of tabs that replace the menu bar.

1. **Title bar**: The title bar appears at the top of all Microsoft applications. It displays the name of the application and current document.

2. **Quick Access Toolbar**: This toolbar is usually displayed at the top-left corner of the screen, but it can be moved further down, below the ribbon. The Quick Access Toolbar

displays some of the commonly used buttons, such as Open, Save, Undo and Quick Print. Buttons can be added and removed by clicking on its drop-down arrow.

3. **Minimize button:** Click on this button to hide the Word window and display whatever is behind it (another Word document if more are open). The document can be retrieved by clicking on its icon on the taskbar at the bottom of the screen.

Above: A view of Microsoft Word 2010 (an example of post-2007 Word) on the PC.

4. **Maximize/Restore button**: If this button shows a single box, then clicking on it will fill the Word page to the full size of the screen (maximize). If two boxes are shown (restore), then clicking on it will reduce the Word screen so other programs and the desktop can be seen.

5. **Close button**: Click on this to close the Word document that is displayed on screen. If there are more Word documents open, these will remain open.

6. **Help**: Activates a help window for information on using Microsoft Word.

7. **Ribbon tabs**: The tabs near the top of the screen which are labelled File, Home, Insert, Page Layout, References, Mailings, Review and View are used to open different ribbons below. These ribbons contain different toolbar buttons associated with each ribbon tab. Word 2007 has an Office button instead of File ribbon tab.

8. **Ribbon**: A ribbon contains a series of buttons, just like a traditional toolbar. Each set of ribbon buttons is associated with its ribbon tab. The ribbon can be minimized and maximized by right clicking on it and selecting the Minimize ribbon (if there's a tick mark against this option, it will maximize).

9. **Horizontal ruler**: Displays the horizontal dimensions (width) of the document in inches or centimetres.

10. **Vertical ruler**: Displays the vertical dimensions (height) of a page in inches or centimetres.

11. **Vertical scroll bar**: Scrolls up and down a document.

12. **Horizontal scroll bar**: Only displayed when the entire width of a page is too wide to be displayed on the screen. Provides left and right scrolling across the document.

13. **Status bar**: Displays the number of pages and the word count for all the text. If some text is selected, a word count for the selected text is also displayed.

14. **Zoom control**: Drag the slider to zoom in and out of the document or click on the + and − symbols. Click on the percentage value to open a Zoom dialogue box and change the settings.

15. **Layouts**: Click on the small buttons to change to different views of the document, including Print Layout, Full Screen Reading, Web Layout, Outline and Draft.

16. **Page up/down**: Scrolls up and down one page at a time.

17. **Vertical split box**: This split box can be used to split or divide the window vertically so that you can view two areas of the document at the same time. Drag the split box down the scroll bar to the position where you want the document to be split.

Hot Tip

Word 2007 doesn't have a File menu ribbon tab. Instead, it has an Office Button, which, when clicked on, displays a list of menu options similar to the File ribbon tab.

THE WORD WINDOW ON MACS

As we have said, most of the information in this book can easily be applied to Apple Macintosh computers too. As you can see from the following two screen shots, they are very similar: the numbered descriptions on pages 30–34 correspond to the annotation here just as well, with only a few minor differences. For example, you'll notice that the name of the current document is just above the ruler, not on the 'title bar', and the 'menu bar' is one and the same as the 'title bar'. See also the note on keyboard differences on page 36.

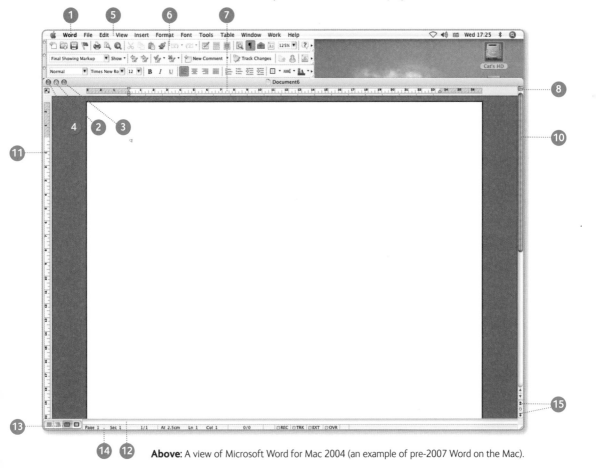

Above: A view of Microsoft Word for Mac 2004 (an example of pre-2007 Word on the Mac).

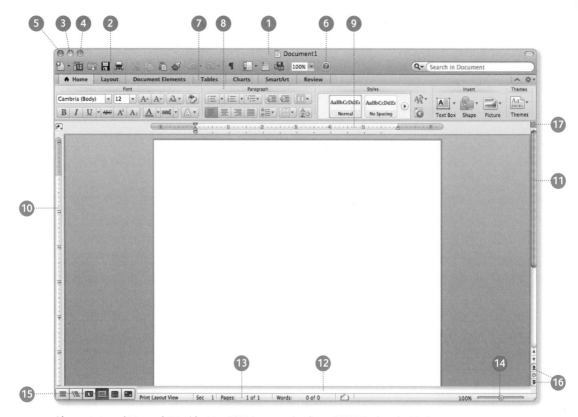

Above: A view of Microsoft Word for Mac 2011 (an example of post-2007 Word on the Mac).

KEYBOARD DIFFERENCES

Any keyboard-related instructions in this book are based on using a keyboard connected to a PC, but – even if you are using a PC – depending on the type of keyboard you are using, you may find some differences. Similarly, if you are using an Apple Mac, there are a few different keys. For example, the Ctrl key on the PC is the Command key on the Apple Mac, despite there being a Ctrl key as well. The Page up/down keys on the PC are usually labelled by an up/down arrow with two short horizontal lines on the Apple Mac. Right clicking is also different on an Apple Mac to the PC: in order to 'right click', hold down the Ctrl key and click, instead.

GETTING STARTED IN WORD

There are lots of shortcuts and quick techniques for opening, closing and saving Word documents and making sure files are not lost. The following section explains the quick methods for accessing Word documents and what to do when files cannot be found.

OPENING AND CLOSING WORD

There are several ways to open Word and there are no right or wrong methods. However, it's worth trying them all to see which one is the quickest and easiest.

Opening Word

➔ **Start menu:** Click on the Start menu at the bottom-left corner of the screen and you may find it listed in the menu that pops up. Otherwise, select Programs or All Programs and look for it on the sub-menu that appears. If it's not there, look for Microsoft Office, select it and look for Word on the next sub-menu.

Above: Some keyboards have a Microsoft Word symbol on a particular key, which can be used to open the program.

➔ **Taskbar:** If Word is displayed as a blue icon (symbol) near the bottom left of the screen, then click on it once with the mouse to open the program.

Above: Microsoft Word is often displayed as a small icon along the bottom of the screen. Click on this icon to open the program.

➔ **Open a Word document**: Instead of opening Word, you can open a Word document (also known as a file), which will automatically open the program. Word documents are usually found via My Computer or My Documents.

Hot Tip

Not sure if Word is open or not? Look along the Taskbar at the bottom of the screen to see if it's displayed. If so, click on it to display the program on screen.

➔ **Keyboard shortcut**: Some keyboards have a Microsoft Word symbol on one of the function keys (for example, F2, as in the picture on page 37), which opens the program. You may have to hold down another key on the keyboard to activate these keyboard features.

Closing Word

➔ **File menu**: Click on the File menu or ribbon tab in Word (the Office button in Word 2007) and select Exit or Close near the bottom of the menu that appears. If any Word documents have not been saved, you will be prompted to save them before the program closes.

Right: Word 2007 doesn't have a File menu or ribbon tab, but a multi-coloured Office button. Click on it to activate a menu with options to open and close documents.

File menu using the keyboard: Hold down the Alt key on the keyboard (near the bottom-left corner of the keyboard), then press F on the keyboard. The File menu or ribbon menu will appear. Release all the keys on the keyboard, then press X for eXit or C for Close. Word will close, but may prompt you to save changes to any unsaved documents.

Close button: At the far top-right corner of the screen there is an X-shaped button. Click on this to close Word. If any Word documents have not been saved, you will be prompted to save them before the program closes. If there is an X-shaped button below the one in the top-right corner of the screen, clicking on this will only close the Word document, not the program.

Above: Click on the X-shaped button in the top-right corner of the Word screen to close the program.

Keyboard shortcut: Hold down the Alt key on the keyboard (near the bottom-left corner of the keyboard) and press the F4 key (above the numbers 4 and 5) once. Word will close, but will ask you to save the changes for any documents that have not been saved.

Right click on the taskbar: When Word is open, it appears on the taskbar along the bottom of the screen. It can be closed from here by right clicking on the taskbar and choosing Close from the menu that appears. If any Word files have not been saved, you will be asked whether you want to save them.

Hot Tip

If you're about to close down your computer and have several programs open, then, providing you've saved any open files, just click on the Start button and choose Turn Off Computer or Shut Down.

OPENING NEW AND OLD WORD DOCUMENTS

Microsoft Word documents or files can be opened and created in a variety of ways via the keyboard, menus, toolbar buttons or a different program.

Creating a New Blank Word Document

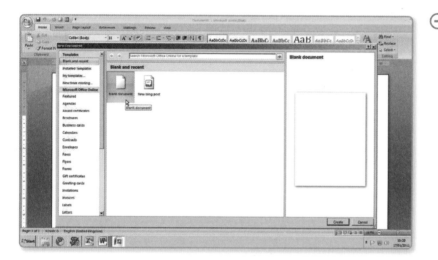

Above: In Word 2007, click on the Office button in the top-left corner of the screen and choose New from the menu that appears. The dialogue box shown here will appear. Select Blank document and click on the Create button to open a new blank document.

→ **Keyboard:** Hold down the Ctrl key on the keyboard (near the bottom-left corner of the keyboard), then press the letter N on the keyboard and release all the keyboard keys. A new Word document (file) will appear on the screen.

→ **Toolbar button (pre-2007):** In Word 2003 and earlier versions, look on the standard toolbar at the top-left corner of the screen for a toolbar button that looks like a white piece of paper with a corner folded over. Click on this once to open a new Word document.

→ **Office button (Word 2007):** Click on the multi-coloured Office button in the top-left corner of the screen and choose New from the menu that appears. A New Document dialogue box will appear. Select Blank document and click on the Create button.

File ribbon (Word 2010): Click on the File ribbon tab near the top left of the screen and choose New from the drop-down menu on the left side of the screen. A variety of options will appear on the screen. Look for Blank document near the top left and select it to open a new document.

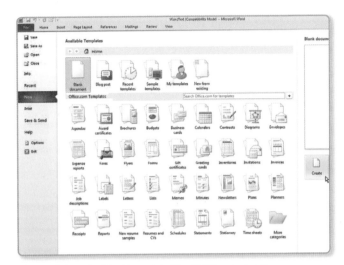

Above: Click on the File ribbon tab in Word 2010 and select New from the menu. The screen shown here will appear. To create a new document, select Blank document, then click on the Create button on the right.

File menu (Word 2002–2003): Click on the File menu and choose New. Look at the right side of the screen at the bar called the Task Pane where details for a New Document will be listed. Select Blank Document and a new blank document will appear in Word.

Above: In Word 2002 and 2003, a new blank document can be created via the Task Pane on the right side of the screen.

File menu (pre-2002): Click on the File menu and choose New. A dialogue box will appear with a variety of options for opening a new document or an assortment of templates. Select Blank Document and click on OK to open a new file in Word.

Opening a Recently Used Word Document

Above: Recently used documents are listed on the File menu in Word 2003 and earlier versions.

➔ **File menu (Word pre-2007):** Click on the File menu and look at the lower half of the menu that appears. The last few Word documents that were opened will be listed. If the file you want is on the list, click on it to open it.

➔ **Office button (Word 2007):** Click on the multi-coloured Office button in the top-left corner of the screen and a list of recently opened Word documents will be displayed, along with a number of menu options.

➔ **File ribbon (Word 2010):** Click on the File ribbon tab near the top-left corner of the screen. From the menu that drops down, select Recent. The files that were last used in Word will be displayed in the main part of the screen. Select one to open it.

Left: Click on the File ribbon tab in Word 2010 and select Recent. Recently opened Word documents will be listed in date order (the most recent are at the top).

➔ **Right click in 2007 and 2010:** With Word open, right click on its icon on the Taskbar along the bottom of the screen. A menu will appear with a section titled Recent, showing the recently used Word documents.

Hot Tip
Recently used files can be listed in Windows XP and earlier versions by clicking on the Start menu at the bottom-left corner of the screen and selecting Documents.

Opening an Old Word Document

The Open dialogue box in Word can be used to locate a Word document and open it. This dialogue box may differ in appearance depending on the version of Word you are using, but the methods of opening folders and selecting a Word document are the same. The following list shows different methods for opening this dialogue box.

1. **Keyboard shortcut:** Hold down the Ctrl key on the keyboard (near the bottom-left corner of the keyboard) and press the letter O on the keyboard (not the zero), then release all the keys on the keyboard. The Open dialogue box will appear on the screen, allowing you to look for a Word document and open it.

2. **File menu (Word pre-2007):** Click on the File menu and choose Open. The Open dialogue box will appear on the screen, allowing you to look for a Word document and open it.

3. **Office button (Word 2007):** Click on the multi-coloured Office button in the top-left corner of the screen and choose Open to activate the Open dialogue box.

4. **File ribbon (Word 2010):** Click on the File ribbon tab at the top left of the screen and choose Open. The Open dialogue box will appear.

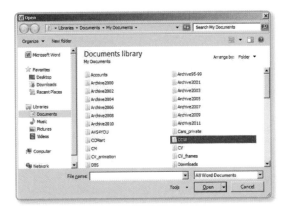

Above: The Open dialogue box can be used to look for and open Word documents.

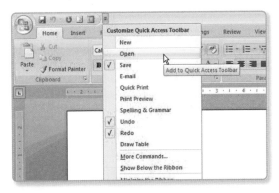

Above: The Quick Access Toolbar in Word 2007 and later versions can display a button to open documents. If this is not shown, it can be added to the toolbar as shown here.

5. **Toolbar button (Word pre-2007):** Look at the top-left corner of the screen along the standard toolbar for a yellow-coloured button (looks like a yellow folder). Hover the mouse pointer over the button and the word Open should appear. Click on the button and the Open dialogue box will appear, enabling you to locate a Word document and open it.

Above: Windows programs including Explorer, My Documents and Documents Library can be used to find and open Word documents.

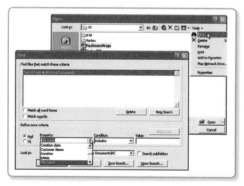

Above: Advanced search facilities for locating Word documents are available via the Open dialogue box.

6. **Quick Access Toolbar (Word 2007–2010):** If a yellow-coloured toolbar button is displayed near the top-left corner of the screen, click on it for the Open dialogue box to appear. If there is no toolbar button, click on the drop-down triangle to the right of these buttons on the Quick Access Toolbar and choose Open from the menu that appears (see the picture on page 43).

Using My Documents and Documents Library to Open Word Documents

If you're familiar with using file viewers such as Windows Explorer, My Computer, My Documents and Documents Library, then any Word document can be opened from here without having to open the program. Instead of opening the program to then open a file, just open the file and Microsoft Word will automatically open with it.

I Can't Remember the Name of a Word File!

When using the Open dialogue box in Word to locate and open a Word document, don't worry if you can't

Hot Tip

Windows has a search facility that can help find lost Word documents. Click on the Start menu and select Search (for Windows 7, type in the search box on the Start menu).

remember the exact name of it. From within the Open dialogue box, there are a number of search methods for finding text within a Word document and finding the author of a file. These are located in the top-right corner of the Open dialogue box. In pre-2007 versions of Word, click on Tools (not the Tools menu in Word) and select Find or Search to open another dialogue box. In Word 2007 and later versions, click inside the search box for a variety of search options.

SAVING

Save your work, don't lose it. Saving and resaving Word documents is quick and easy with keyboard shortcuts and toolbar buttons. It's good practice to regularly save your Word documents, but if a computer problem occurs, Word has some recovery methods to ensure all is not lost.

Saving a Word Document for the First Time

If you are working on a new Word document, which hasn't been saved before, then you will need to save and name it. The quickest way to do this is to hold down the Ctrl key on the keyboard and press the letter S on the keyboard.

Hot Tip

The name of a Word document can consist of several words with spaces between the words, making it easier to understand.

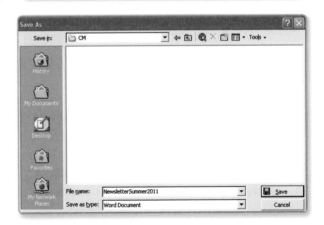

Above: When a Word document is saved for the first time, a Save As dialogue box appears.

Above: In Word 2007 and later versions, a Save button is usually displayed on the Quick Access Toolbar. This is useful for saving and resaving a document.

A Save As dialogue box will appear, allowing you to enter a name for your Word document and choose a location to save it.

Resaving Word Documents

Whilst working on a Word document, it's worthwhile resaving the file every few minutes to avoid losing data if a computer problem occurs. Resaving allows Word to save the current document with all its changes. Here are two methods for quickly resaving a Word document:

➔ **Keyboard shortcut:** Hold down the Ctrl key on the keyboard and press the letter S. You won't see much happening (a brown floppy disk symbol may quickly appear near the bottom of the screen), but the file will have been saved.

➔ **Toolbar button:** Click on the Save toolbar button near the top left of the screen. It looks like a floppy disk and the word Save will appear if you hover over it. In Word 2007 and later versions, this button is on the Quick Access Toolbar, whereas in previous versions of Word it's on the standard toolbar.

Hot Tip

Filenames can be quickly renamed within My Documents, Windows Explorer and Documents Library. Just select a file, press F2 on the keyboard and type a new name for the file.

Changing the Name of a Word Document

If you want to change the name of a Word document or save a copy of it with a different name, then this can be completed within Word. With the file you want to rename open in Word, press F12 on the keyboard and the Save As dialogue box will appear. Enter a new name for your Word document and, if required, choose a different location in which to store it. Click on the Save button and the Word document will be resaved with a new name. The old Word document will not be overwritten.

Word .doc and .docx Extensions

All filenames have an extension to help identify the program in which the file can be used. This usually consists of three or four letters at the end of the filename and is separated from the filename with a full stop (for example, Newsletter.doc). Pre-2007 versions of Word use a .doc extension at the end of the filename, whereas documents created in Word 2007 and later versions have a .docx extension.

Why Have Different Extensions?

Surely it would be easier to use the same file extension, no matter which version of Microsoft Word you are using? Unfortunately, this is not so easy, because some of the features used within a Word file created in version 2010, for instance, are not available in an earlier version such as Word 97. Consequently, different file extensions are used in Word 2007–2010 to help differentiate.

Above: A document created in Word 2007 or a later version of the program will have a .docx extension to the filename (for example, Letterhead.docx).

Saving a Word Document to Open in an Earlier Version

If you want to transfer a Word document to another computer where an earlier version of the program is available, the file can be resaved to ensure it can be opened. With the file in question open in Word, press F12 on the keyboard.

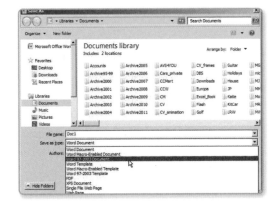

Right: A Word document can be saved as a different file type, making it easier to open in an older version of the program.

The Save As dialogue box will appear. Click on the drop-down triangle to the right of the Save as type or File type box. A list of file types will appear. From here you can choose Word 97–2003 Document, for example. After choosing a file type, you can rename the file or keep the same name and select a location to store the file, then click on the Save button.

OPENING .DOCX FILES IN WORD 97-2003

A compatibility pack that allows Word documents with a .docx extension, which were created in Word 2007 or later, to be opened by Word 97–2003 can be downloaded from http://support.microsoft.com/kb/924074.

CLOSING WORD DOCUMENTS WITHOUT CLOSING WORD

- **File menu/tab**: Click on the File menu, Office button or ribbon tab and choose Close.

- **X-button**: If there are two X-shaped buttons in the top-right corner of the Word screen, click on the lower button to close the file (the upper button closes Word). If there's only one X-shaped button, click on this to close the Word document.

Hot Tip

If you have several files open in Word 2003 or an earlier version and want to close them all without closing Word, hold down the shift key on the keyboard, then click on the File menu and choose Close All.

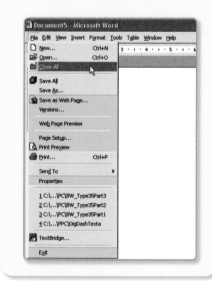

Hot Tip

Press Ctrl+W on the keyboard to close a Word document without closing the program.

CRASH RECOVERY

If Word develops a problem and has to close, a warning box will usually appear before the program closes. After Word has closed, it may open again (for earlier versions, you may have to reopen Word) and the file(s) you were working on will reappear as recovered files. You will then have a choice to resave them without losing any changes. Word can recover files when the program has to close, because it uses an auto recovery feature that automatically saves any open documents at regular intervals.

Modifying Auto Recovery in Word Pre-2007

Click on the Tools menu and choose Options. From the dialogue box that appears, select the Save tab and look for the words 'Save AutoRecover info every:'. There will be a number next to this, which represents minutes and can be altered.

Modifying Auto Recovery in Word 2007 and Later Versions

In Word 2007, click on the Office button in the top-left corner of the screen and choose Word Options, or in Word 2010, click on the File ribbon tab and choose Options. In both cases a dialogue box will appear. Choose Save from the list on the left and look for the AutoRecover information, where the value in minutes can be changed.

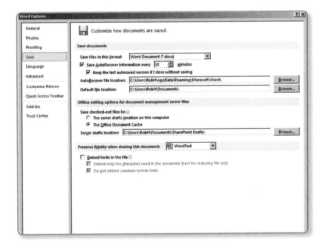

Above: The frequency by which a Word document's information is saved for auto recovery and its location can be changed via the Options dialogue box in Word 2007–2010.

MOVING AROUND A DOCUMENT

It can be hard work to scroll through hundreds of pages in a document and find the text you are looking for. However, there are several keyboard and on-screen shortcuts to save hours of frustration and make navigating through a document quick and easy.

QUICK MOVES WITH THE KEYBOARD

Ctrl+Home: The cursor moves to the beginning of the document.

Ctrl+End: The cursor moves to the end of the document.

Home: The cursor moves to the beginning of the line.

End: The cursor moves to the end of the line.

Page up/down: The cursor moves up or down one whole screen page at a time.

Ctrl+down/up arrow: The cursor moves up or down one paragraph at a time.

Hot Tip

When using the Ctrl key with another key, always hold down the Ctrl key first before pressing the other key.

SCROLLING

The scroll bars on screen and the scroll wheel on the mouse can all be used to move quickly through a document.

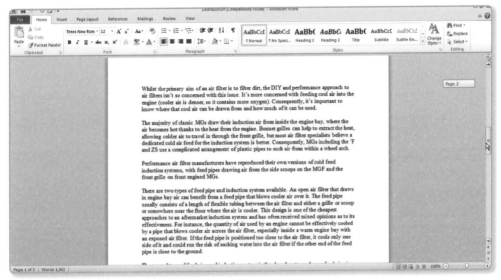

Above: Dragging the scroll marker is a quick way of moving through a long document. Notice the page number is displayed near the scroll marker whilst dragging it.

Scroll Bars

The vertical scroll bar is always displayed on the screen, whereas the horizontal scroll bar is only displayed when the width of the page cannot fit on the screen. These scroll bars can be used as follows:

- **Drag the marker:** The scroll bar marker shows the current position in the document. Drag this marker to quickly move up and down or across the document.

- **Click next to the marker:** Scroll one screen page up, down or across by clicking next to the scroll bar marker, inside the scroll bar.

Hot Tip

When dragging the vertical scroll bar marker, the page number to which you are moving will be displayed next to it.

➔ **Click on the arrows:** Click on the arrows (triangles) at the ends of the scroll bars to scroll up, down or across the document. This is one of the traditional techniques and the slowest method.

Hot Tip

Click the scroll wheel to switch on horizontal and vertical scrolling. The mouse pointer will change and can be moved away from the centre of the screen to begin scrolling. Click the scroll wheel again to switch this off.

Scroll Wheel

If your mouse has a scroll wheel, this can be used to move quickly around a document. If there is only one scroll wheel, this can be used to scroll up and down a document by rotating it. If there is a second scroll wheel, it can often be used to scroll across a document.

Quick Zoom with a Scroll Wheel

In some cases, a vertical scroll wheel on a mouse can be used to zoom in and out of a document. Hold down the Ctrl key on the keyboard, then rotate the vertical scroll wheel. The screen should zoom in and out.

BROWSING

Navigating through a document can often be easier using the Browse Objects feature. This is displayed near the bottom-right corner of the screen and looks like a small ball with double-headed arrows above and below it. Click on the small ball and a palette of small icons will appear (hover over them to see what they can do).

Hot Tip

Open the Browse Objects palette by holding down the Ctrl and Alt keys on the keyboard, then pressing the Home key. The palette will appear in the bottom-right corner of the screen.

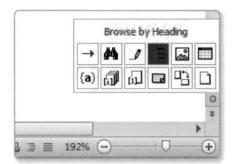

Above: Browse by Heading to quickly move between headings in a Word document.

Browse by Heading

If a document contains several headings (such as Heading 1, Heading 2, Heading 3), Word can quickly move up or down them. Choose the Browse by Heading option on the Browse Objects palette, then click on the double-headed arrow buttons above or below the Browse Objects button. Word will move up or down the document to the next heading.

Find Text

Text can be quickly found in a Word document by using the Find facility. This can be opened via the Browse Objects button, by clicking on the Find button on the palette. A Find dialogue box will appear. Type some text to look for, then click on the Find Next button. If Word finds the text, it will move to its location in the document and highlight it. If no text is found or Word reaches the end of the document, a message box will appear.

Right: The Find features in the Navigation pane in Word 2007 and later versions provide a useful list of easy-to-understand results.

Hot Tip

Hold down the Ctrl key on the keyboard and press F to open Word's Find facility. In Word 2007 and later versions, this opens a larger search panel displayed down the left side of the screen.

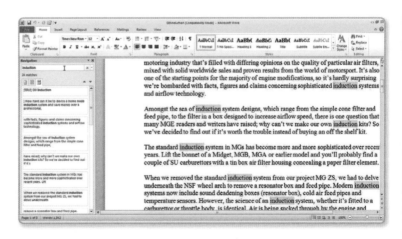

CREATING A DOCUMENT

STARTING WITH A NEW OR EXISTING DOCUMENT

There are several approaches to creating a document in Word and lots of time-saving techniques that can save hours of typing. The following section explains how to use blank documents, templates and existing files.

USING A BLANK DOCUMENT

Chapter one covered in-depth instructions on starting Microsoft Word and using a blank document. When Microsoft Word is opened, a blank document is instantly created, making it quick and easy to start typing. However, there are some pre-made documents called templates that can save hours of typing.

What Is a Template?

A template is a ready-made document containing text, images and other information that can be used. It can save a lot of time and typing, and is useful for creating letters, faxes, expense claim forms and reports where reusable headings, paragraphs of text and images have already been

Left: Word has a large assortment of templates that can save hours of repetitive typing.

entered. A template is similar to an original copy of a document, which can be photocopied time and time again without marking the original.

Where Are Word's Templates?

Word has a selection of templates supplied with the program and stored on your computer, plus many more are available via the Internet. To see the templates available and use them, click on the File menu or ribbon tab (click on the Office button in Word 2007) and select New. A dialogue box will appear with some templates and categories of templates (depending on the version of Word). To use one, select it and click on Create, Open or OK. A new document will be created and contain the contents of the template.

Hot Tip

The Open dialogue box can be quickly activated by holding down the Ctrl key on the keyboard and pressing the letter O.

USING AN OLD FILE

One popular method of creating a document in Word is to use the contents of an old document. Whilst this is almost the same as a template, many people open an old document, then resave it with a different name. However, Word has a quicker solution. Locate and select the Word document using the Open dialogue box, then click on the drop-down triangle next to the Open button. From the menu that drops down, select Open as Copy. A copy of the document will be opened, leaving the original intact.

Above: If you want to create a document based on the contents of another document, this can be done using the Open dialogue box.

TYPING AND FORMATTING TEXT

Text can be quickly typed into a document in Microsoft Word, but changing the look of that text and how it's presented can take a lot longer if you don't know the quick techniques and shortcuts. The following pages reveal the popular enhancements used to change the look of text in a Word document.

STANDARD SETTINGS

Word uses some default settings when creating a document and enabling text to be typed. For instance, a new document usually begins with an A4 portrait-shaped page with single line spacing. The text is usually aligned to the left side of the page, written in the font Times New Roman at a size of size 11 in black. However, there are so many other settings for the presentation of the text and the size of the page.

CHANGING THE FONT, COLOUR AND SIZE

Common attributes including the type of font used in a piece of text, its size and colour can all be changed using the toolbar buttons. These buttons are found on the Formatting toolbar in Word 2003 and earlier versions, or on the Home ribbon tab in Word 2007 and later versions.

Hot Tip

If the Formatting toolbar has disappeared in Word 2003 or an earlier version, right click on the menu bar or another toolbar and make sure there's a tick mark against Formatting from the shortcut menu that appears.

Font Dialogue Box

A Font dialogue box provides an extensive choice of font settings (type, colours, size). This dialogue box can be opened in Word 2003 and earlier versions by clicking on the Format menu and choosing Font. In Word 2007 and later

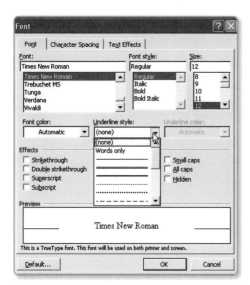

Above: The Font dialogue box can be used to make several changes to text.

Hot Tip

The Font dialogue box can be opened by holding down the Ctrl key and pressing D on the keyboard.

versions, click on the Home ribbon tab, look for the Font ribbon set and click on the small box and arrow in the bottom-right corner of this group of buttons.

Default Font Settings

Each Word document has a number of settings for standard text (known as Normal), which relate to the type of font, its size, colour and other attributes. These settings can be changed from within the Font dialogue box. Select the font, size and colour you want to use throughout the document, then click on the button labelled Set As Default or Default.

Hot Tip

Increase or reduce the size of a font by holding down the Ctrl and Shift keys, then pressing the > key to make the font size larger, or the < key to make it smaller. This also works for selected text.

ADDING BOLD, UNDERLINE AND ITALICS

Popular font attributes, such as bold, underline and italics can be set via the Font dialogue box or using the toolbar buttons on the Formatting toolbar (Word pre-2007) or Home ribbon tab (Word 2007 and later). However, there is a quicker way of setting these attributes, using the following keyboard shortcuts (press the relevant keys to switch on, say, bold, and press them again to switch it off):

- **Bold**: Ctrl+B.
- **Italics**: Ctrl+I.
- **Underline**: Ctrl+U.
- **Double underline**: Ctrl+Shift+D.

CHANGING ALIGNMENT

Text is usually justified to the left side of the page in Word. This can be changed by selecting one of the justification buttons on the formatting toolbar (Word 2003 and earlier versions) or the Paragraph ribbon on the Home ribbon tab (Word 2007 and later). However, the following shortcut keys are even quicker:

- **Left align a paragraph**: Ctrl+L.

- **Right align a paragraph**: Ctrl+R (press these keys again and the paragraph switches back to being left aligned).

- **Centre a paragraph**: Ctrl+E (press these keys again and the paragraph switches back to being left aligned).

- **Left and right justify a paragraph**: Ctrl+J (press these keys again and the paragraph switches back to being left aligned).

Hot Tip

Change text to the default font settings by selecting it, then holding down the Ctrl key on the keyboard and pressing the space-bar.

WRITING IN COLUMNS

Text can be written and presented in a newspaper style with two or more columns on the page. The text runs down the first column on the far left of the page,

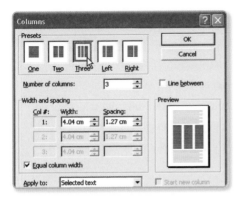

Left: The Columns dialogue box allows the number of columns to be set for selected text or for an entire document.

then continues at the top of the second column. Existing text can be converted to columns by selecting it first, or the columns can be set before the text is typed. In both cases, the following instructions outline how to set up the columns:

➔ **Word 2003 and earlier versions:** Click on the Format menu and choose Columns. From the dialogue box that appears, select the number of columns, whether you need spacing and if the columns have to be applied to the whole document or the selected text. Click on OK to apply the columns.

➔ **Word 2007 and later versions:** Click on the Page Layout ribbon tab and select the Columns button near the top-left corner of the screen. A choice of columns will drop down in a menu, but if you need further options, select More Columns and a dialogue box will appear with more settings.

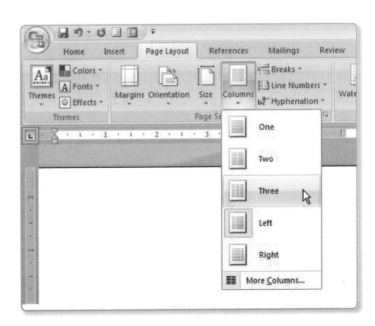

Right: Columns can be set via the Page Layout ribbon tab in Word 2007 and later versions.

LINE SPACING

Most Word documents use single line spacing between each line of text in a paragraph (this is often different to the space before and after a paragraph). However, this can be changed to one and a half, double and other settings. One method for setting line spacing is to select the text where the line spacing needs changing, right click inside the selected text and choose Paragraph from the shortcut menu that appears. A Paragraph dialogue box will appear, displaying settings for line spacing. Alternatively, the following shortcut keys can quickly set line spacing:

- **Single:** Ctrl+1.
- **Double:** Ctrl+2.
- **1.5-lines:** Ctrl+5.

PARAGRAPH PROBLEMS

Sometimes, Word will add an unwanted or extra-large line space before or after a paragraph. This can be reduced or increased by selecting the paragraph of text and right clicking inside it. From the shortcut menu that appears, select Paragraph and a dialogue box will appear. Look at the settings in the lower half of this dialogue box, under Spacing. Change the values against Before and After to increase or reduce the height of space before and after the paragraph.

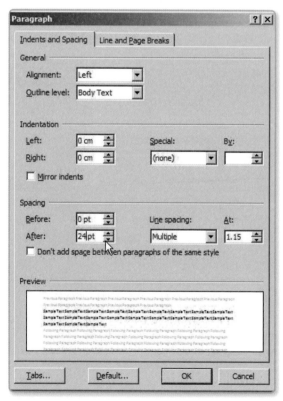

Above: Line spacing before or after a paragraph can sometimes become annoying. However, it can be adjusted via the Paragraph dialogue box.

SELECTING TEXT

If you can select text quickly, the time spent manipulating paragraphs and editing sentences can easily be halved. Keyboard shortcuts and fast techniques with the mouse can save time selecting text. The following section shows the fastest methods to help reduce time and ease frustration.

MOUSE SELECTION

The mouse makes selecting text quick and easy. In most cases, the fastest technique for selecting text is to hold the left button down on the mouse and swipe the mouse pointer across the text. However, there are instances where this can be difficult, so here are a few faster methods for selecting text with the mouse:

- **Double click**: Double click on a word and the entire word will be selected.

- **Triple click**: Perform three left clicks over a word and the entire paragraph will be selected.

- **Click from the side**: Move the mouse pointer to the left side of the text and when it changes to a white arrow pointing up to the right, left-click the mouse once to select the adjacent line of text (*see* the picture at the top of the page overleaf).

- **Double click from the side**: Move the mouse pointer to the left side of the text and when it changes to a white arrow pointing up to the right, click twice with the left button to select the entire paragraph next to the mouse pointer (*see* the picture overleaf).

- **Triple click from the side**: Move the mouse pointer to the left side of the text and when it changes to a white arrow pointing up to the right, click three times with the left button to select all the text in the document.

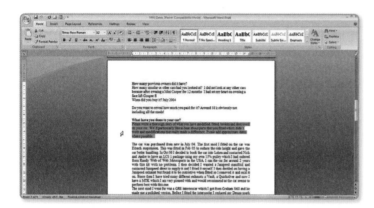

Above: Move the mouse pointer to the left of the text and when it changes to a white arrow, single click to select the adjacent line of text, or double click to select the entire paragraph.

Ctrl+click: Hold down the Ctrl key, then swipe over some text to select it. Release the left button, but keep the Ctrl key held down, then move to some other text and select it. The first block of selected text will remain selected. Repeat this procedure to select more unconnected blocks of text.

Alt+swipe: Selects part of a document, irrespective of content. Hold down the Alt key on the keyboard, then keep the left button held down on the mouse and move down and across the screen to select a section of the document. Notice that the pattern of the selection isn't affected by the structure of the text.

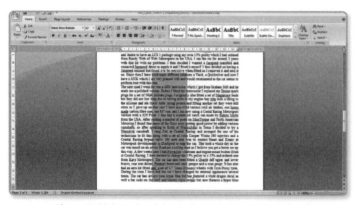

Above: Hold down the Alt key and swipe over an area inside a document to select it. This method of selection can be useful for tabbed text.

Shift+click: Position the cursor at the beginning of the block of text you want to select. Move the mouse pointer (do not left click with it) to the point in the text where you want to end the selection (you may need to scroll down the screen). Hold down the Shift key on the keyboard, then left click once to select all of the text from where the cursor was positioned to the mouse pointer.

KEYBOARD SELECTION

Text can be quickly selected in a document using the keys on the keyboard, making it quicker to move, copy or delete words, sentences or paragraphs. The following keyboard shortcuts can save hours of editing time:

- **Ctrl+Shift+left/right arrow key**: Selects a word to the left/right of the cursor.

- **Ctrl+Shift+up/down arrow key**: Selects a paragraph of text.

- **Shift+Home/End**: Selects all the text from the cursor to the beginning (Home key) or end (End key) of the line.

- **Ctrl+Shift+Home/End**: Selects all the text from the cursor to the beginning (Home key) or end (End key) of the document.

- **Shift+Page up/down**: Selects a full screen of text above (Page up) or below (Page down) the cursor.

- **Ctrl+A**: Selects all the text in a document.

DELETING, MOVING AND COPYING TEXT

Changing, deleting, moving and copying text is one of the most important aspects of a word processor, but if you don't know the shortcuts and quick techniques, it can become very time consuming. The following pages show how to save time when editing text.

DELETING TEXT

There are two keyboard keys that remove text from a document: the Delete key and the Backspace key (above the Enter or Return key). Removing large sections of text can take a long time unless the Delete or Backspace keys are used with other combinations of keys.

Ctrl Deleting

Hold down the Ctrl key and press Delete once to remove an entire word. This method will delete the word that follows the cursor. If you want to delete the word before the cursor, hold down the Ctrl key and press the Backspace key once.

Select and Delete

In the previous section of this chapter there are detailed instructions on quick techniques for selecting paragraphs and blocks of text. Once some text has been selected, press Delete on the keyboard to remove it from the document.

MOVING THROUGH TEXT

It can become very frustrating moving up and down a document using the keyboard, especially using the arrow keys. However, there are some shortcuts that can save time:

- **Ctrl+left/right arrow keys**: Hold down the Ctrl key on the keyboard and press the left or right arrow key to jump one word at a time.

- **Ctrl+up/down arrow keys**: Hold down the Ctrl key on the keyboard and press the up or down arrow keys on the keyboard to jump one paragraph at a time.

- **Home/End**: Moves the cursor to the beginning or end of a line of text.

- **Ctrl+ Home/End**: Moves the cursor to the beginning or end of a document.

- **Page up/down**: Moves the cursor up or down one full screen of the document.

MOVING TEXT

Text can be quickly and easily moved along a line, to another paragraph or even to another document. There are a number of quick techniques to do this.

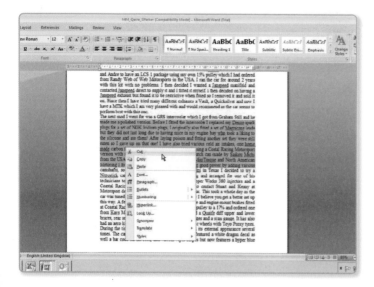

Left: Text can be moved by selecting it, then right clicking inside the selection and choosing Cut. Right click elsewhere and choose Paste to move it.

Cut and Paste

The most traditional method for moving text is to cut and paste it. This involves selecting the text, then doing one of the following to cut it (the selected text will disappear from the document, but will reappear when it's pasted):

➡ **Right click:** Right click inside the selected text and a shortcut menu will appear. Choose Cut from the menu.

➡ **Ctrl+X:** Hold down the Ctrl key on the keyboard and press the letter X to cut the selected text.

➡ **Cut toolbar button:** The Cut toolbar button looks like a pair of scissors and is on the standard toolbar in Word 2003 and earlier versions, or the Home ribbon tab in Word 2007 and later versions.

➡ **Edit menu:** In Word 2003 and earlier versions, click on the Edit menu and choose Cut.

Fast Paste Techniques

Pasting is just as quick as cutting and involves similar techniques to the aforementioned methods of cutting. For example, you can right click and choose Paste, press Ctrl+V, use the Paste toolbar button or, in Word 2003 and earlier versions, click on the Edit menu and choose Paste.

Dragging Text

One of the quickest methods of moving text around inside a document is to select and drag it. Once the text has been selected, position the mouse pointer inside this selection and it will change to a white arrow. When this happens, hold the left button down and move the mouse pointer to start moving the text. Nothing much will happen, but move the mouse pointer to the new location for the text (you may see a faint vertical line). Release the left button to move the selected text.

> ## Hot Tip
> **Text can be copied when dragging it. Just hold down the Ctrl key and release the mouse button first.**

COPYING TEXT

The methods for copying and pasting text are similar to cutting and pasting. The following techniques are some of the most popular:

➔ **Right click**: Right click inside the selected text and a shortcut menu will appear. Choose Copy from the menu. Right click on the location where the text is to be pasted, then choose Paste from the menu.

➔ **Ctrl+C**: Hold down the Ctrl key on the keyboard and press the letter C to copy the selected text. Position the cursor at the point where the text is to be pasted, then hold down the Ctrl key and press the letter V to paste the copied text.

➔ **Copy toolbar button**: The Copy toolbar button looks like two pieces of paper and is on the standard toolbar in

Word 2003 and earlier versions, or the Home ribbon tab in Word 2007 and later versions. Click on it to copy some selected text, position the cursor where the text is to be pasted, then click on the Paste toolbar button.

 Edit menu: In Word 2003 and earlier versions, click on the Edit menu and choose Copy to take a copy of some selected text. Position the cursor at the point where the text is to be pasted, then return to the Edit menu and select Paste.

COPYING WITH THE CLIPBOARD

When Word 2002 was released, it included a clipboard that could be used across the entire Office 2002 suite of programs, including Outlook, Word and PowerPoint. This allowed up to 24 items to be copied and listed on the clipboard, then pasted into different programs.

Using the Clipboard in Word 2002 and 2003

The Clipboard is displayed down the right side of the screen and can be opened by clicking on the Edit menu and choosing Office Clipboard. When some text, a table, an object or an image are copied, they are listed in the Clipboard with the most recent at the top. To paste an item from the Clipboard into Word, position the cursor where the item is to be copied to, then click on the item listed in the Clipboard.

Using the Clipboard in Word 2007 and 2010

The Clipboard is displayed down the left side of the screen and can be opened by selecting the Home ribbon tab and clicking on Clipboard near the top left of the screen. When several pieces of text are copied, they are listed in the Clipboard with the most recent at the top. To paste an item from the Clipboard into Word, select the appropriate cell, then click on the item listed in the Clipboard.

Removing Items from the Clipboard

Hover the mouse pointer over a copied item that is listed in the Clipboard. A box will appear around it with a drop-down triangle to the right. Click on this drop-down triangle and a short menu will appear with the option to delete the entry. Click on Delete to remove the item from the Clipboard.

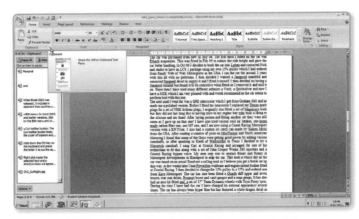

Above: Word 2007 and later versions display a Clipboard down the left side of the screen, which can store up to 24 copied items.

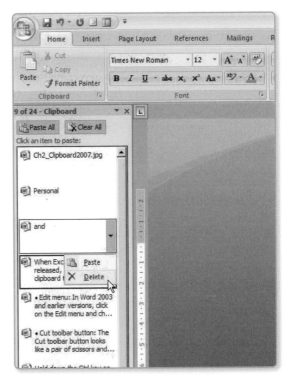

Hot Tip

To remove all the items listed in the Clipboard, click on the Clear All button near the top of it.

Right: Copied items can be removed from the Clipboard by selecting their respective drop-down triangle or arrow and choosing Delete from the menu that appears.

Above: The Smart Tag for paste options appears after pasting text or an object into a Word document. It can help to change the look of the copied item.

COPY ERRORS

Sometimes, text can be copied but the pasted text needs to be altered. In Word 2002 and later versions, a Smart Tag appears next to the pasted text. Click on this tag and a short menu will appear with some options for altering the look (format) of the text. The Smart Tag is known as Paste Options in Word 2007 and later versions.

Paste Special

All versions of Microsoft Word use Paste Special, which can help to correctly paste copied text, objects or images into a Word document. After copying something, position the cursor at the point where the text, object or image has to be pasted. In Word 2003 and earlier versions, click on the Edit menu and choose Paste Special. In later versions of Word, select the Home ribbon tab, click on the drop-down triangle below the Paste button (top-right corner of the screen) and choose Paste Special. From the dialogue box that appears, here are some of the useful options to consider:

➔ **Formatted text (RTF):**
Retains the original formatting.

➔ **Unformatted text:** Removes
all formatting.

➔ **HTML format:** Useful for
copying text from a web page
and keeping the formatting.

➔ **Microsoft Excel chart
object:** Useful for copying
and pasting a chart from
Excel into Word.

➔ **Paste link:** This option button is
usually on the left side of the
dialogue box and provides an up-to-
date link to the copied text or object,
so if the original is changed, the
copied text or object in the Word
document will also change.

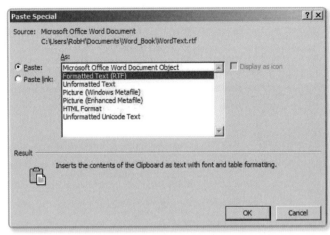

Above: The Paste Special dialogue box can often enable text and
objects to be correctly copied and pasted into a Word document.

Hot Tip

**If a Paste Special doesn't look as good as
expected, the action can be quickly undone
straight away by holding down the Ctrl key and
pressing Z (this is known as undo).**

STEP-BY-STEP: COPY TEXT FROM THE INTERNET

If text is copied from a website and pasted into Word, it is often displayed with the wrong font
and in an unsuitable colour. Plus, many virus checkers will assess any copied text from the
Internet when it is pasted, which delays the copy–paste process and it will seem as though the
computer is running slowly. The following steps show how to correctly copy–paste text from a
website into Word.

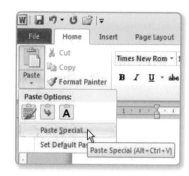

Hot Tip

In Word 2007–2010, press Ctrl+Alt+V to open the Paste Special dialogue box; this only works after something has been copied.

1. Select the text on the web page that needs to be copied by holding the left button down and swiping across with the mouse. Right click inside the selected text and choose Copy. If this does not work, hold down the Ctrl key on the keyboard and press C. The selected text will now be copied.

Above: Paste Special is found on the drop-down menu in the top-left corner of the screen in Word 2007–2010.

2. Position the cursor at the point in a Word document where the copied text should be displayed. In Word pre-2007, click on the Edit menu and choose Paste Special. In Word 2007–2010, click on the Home ribbon tab, select the drop-down arrow underneath the Paste button (top-left corner of the screen) and choose Paste Special. In all cases, the Paste Special dialogue box will appear.

3. With the Paste Special dialogue box displayed on screen, select Unformatted Text from the list. This will ensure the copied text is inserted into the Word document without any formatting. Click on OK to close this dialogue box and return to the Word document.

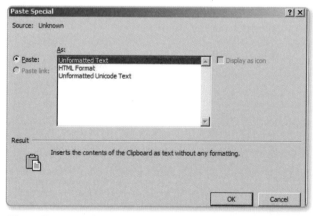

Above: Choosing Unformatted Text within the Paste Special dialogue box ensures that anything that is copied into Word is stripped of its formatting.

4. If the formatting of the copy–pasted text is wrong, select all of the text, then either change the font and other settings using the toolbar or ribbon buttons, or hold down the Ctrl key on the keyboard and press the space-bar (this will reset its formatting).

COPYING FONTS AND OTHER FORMATTING

If the formatting of some text is wrong, but correct in other parts of a document, the correct formatting can be copied into the text where the formatting is incorrect. This is known as the Format Painter in Word. In Word 2007 and later versions, it can be found on the Home ribbon tab, in the top-left corner of the screen. In earlier versions of Word, the Format Painter is a toolbar button near the Cut, Copy and Paste buttons.

Using the Format Painter

Select a word or block of text that is correctly formatted. Click once on the Format Painter button to copy the formatting of the selected text. Next, use the mouse to select the text that needs to be changed to the correct formatting. The formatting of this text will change and will be the same as the text that was first selected.

Multiple Format Painting

When selecting the Format Painter button, double click on it to permanently switch it on. You can now select several blocks of text with the mouse and each one will have its formatting changed. To switch off the Format Painter, press Escape on the keyboard or click a second time on the Format Painter button.

Above: After selecting the Format Painter button, the mouse pointer changes shape and has a brush attached to it when hovering over text.

CHANGING THE VIEW

The on-screen view of a Word document can sometimes be difficult to scroll through and make it hard to find specific text. There are, however, plenty of time-saving techniques, including a full screen view, changing the zoom controls, splitting the screen and viewing more than one document at a time. These useful methods are explained over the following pages.

WHAT YOU SEE IS WHAT YOU GET (WYSIWYG)

One of the most popular screen views for a Word document is Print Layout because it shows how each page will look when printed. Each page that is displayed on screen can show all four edges and corners, so you can instantly see all four margins and the position of text, tables and images. There are a few ways to select Print Layout, which are outlined as follows:

- **Print Layout button:** Click on the Print Layout button near the bottom-left or bottom-right corner of the screen (depending on the version of Word).

- **View menu:** In Word 2003 and earlier versions, click on the View menu and choose Print Layout.

- **View ribbon tab:** For Word 2007 and later versions, click on the View ribbon tab and select the Print Layout button near the top-left corner of the screen.

FULL SCREEN VIEW

Sometimes, the menus, ribbons and toolbar buttons are not used in Word, especially when text is being proofread or there's a lot of text to type. Consequently, it may be easier to hide all of these buttons and menus so the text can fill as much of the screen as possible. This can be achieved in a number of ways, depending on the version of Word.

Full Screen Reading in Word 2007-2010

Word 2007 and later versions have a view called Full Screen Reading, which maximizes the view of the document and displays it like a book with two pages side by side on the screen. Click on the View ribbon tab and select the Full Screen Reading button near the top-left

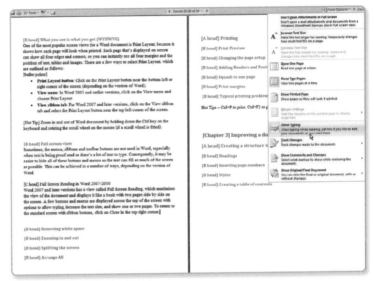

Above: Full Screen Reading in Word 2007 and later versions allows reading and editing of a document with the minimum amount of buttons and menus cluttering up the screen.

corner of the screen. In Full Screen Reading, a few buttons and menus are displayed across the top of the screen with options to allow typing, increase the text size and show one or two pages. To switch off Full Screen Reading, click on Close in the top-right corner.

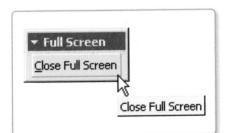

Above: The full screen view in Word 2003 and earlier versions can be closed by clicking on the toolbar button shown here. If this is not displayed, press Escape on the keyboard instead.

Full Screen

Word 2003 and earlier versions uses a Full Screen option found on the View menu. This removes the toolbars, menus, title bar and scroll bars, allowing as much of the document as possible to be viewed on screen. A small floating box is displayed on screen with the option to Close Full Screen. If this box is accidentally closed or doesn't appear, press Escape on the keyboard to close the full screen view.

HIDING WHITE SPACE

Word 2002 and later versions can reduce the amount of unused space in Print Layout view between the bottom of one page and the top of the next page. This helps to reduce the amount of time spent scrolling up and down through pages. To hide this unused space (it's called white space), make sure the Print Layout view is on screen, then position the mouse pointer in the gap between two pages. When the mouse pointer changes to two boxes and arrows with the label Hide White Space, left click once. The gap will disappear and be replaced by a thick black line.

Above: The unused space between the bottom of a page and the top of the next page can be hidden to make it faster to scroll through pages in a document.

Retrieving White Space

Position the mouse pointer over the thick black line that represents the dividing line between two pages. The mouse pointer will change to two boxes and arrows with the label Show White Space. Left click once to unhide the white space. There will now be a gap between the two pages.

OTHER USEFUL VIEWS

The following list provides details on some of the other views available in Word and how they can be used:

- **Normal or Draft view:** This view doesn't show how the text will be printed on to a page and doesn't show the margins around the page. Pages are divided by a faint dotted line. Normal view was replaced by Draft view in Word 2007. Both views are useful for typing text that won't be printed.

- **Web layout:** Useful if a Word document is going to be converted into a web page. This is covered more in depth in chapter five.

● **Outline view**: If headings are used throughout a document, then the Outline view can help to see a list of the headings to examine the structure and content of the document.

ZOOMING IN AND OUT

The view of a Word document can be enlarged or reduced to help see more pages or read the text. This is known as zooming and there are various methods for zooming in and out of a document. The following points explain the most popular:

● **Ctrl+scroll wheel**: This is the quickest method of zooming in and out, but you will need a mouse with a scroll wheel. Hold down the Ctrl key on the keyboard and rotate the scroll wheel to zoom in or out. This technique works in many other programs.

● **View–Zoom**: In Word 2003 and earlier versions, click on the View menu and choose Zoom. In later versions of Word, click on the View ribbon tab, then select the Zoom button. In both cases, a Zoom dialogue box will appear, which provides a number of options for increasing or reducing the view of the document.

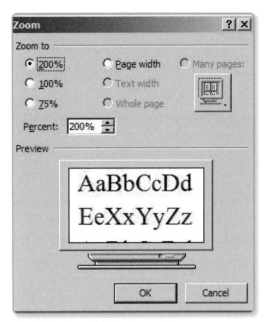

Above: The Zoom dialogue box provides various settings to enlarge or reduce the view of the document on the screen.

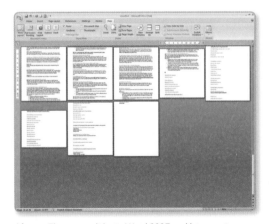

Above: The zoom slider in Word 2007 and later versions provides a quick method of zooming in and out of a document to be able to see one or all of the pages.

Zoom slider: Word 2007 and later versions have some Zoom controls in the bottom-right corner of the screen. Drag the slider to zoom in or out of the document. Click on the % zoom value to open the Zoom dialogue box.

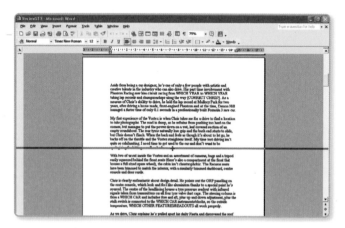

Above: When the split screen is activated, the mouse pointer jumps to the middle of the screen and a horizontal line appears.

SPLITTING THE SCREEN

Sometimes, you need to see two different sections of a document (for example, notes at the top and the main text at the bottom). Word can provide two separate views of a document, which can both be edited, by horizontally splitting the screen. The following points explain how to split the screen in different versions of Word:

Word pre-2007: Click on the Window menu and choose Split. The mouse pointer will jump to the middle of the screen and a line will be drawn across the screen. Move the mouse pointer up and down to adjust the split, then left click once to set it.

Word 2007 and later versions: Click on the View ribbon tab and select the Split button in the top middle of the screen. The mouse

Hot Tip

A split screen button is positioned above the up arrow on the vertical scroll bar. Drag it down the screen to activate the split screen.

pointer will jump to the middle of the screen and a line will be drawn across the screen. Move the mouse pointer up and down to adjust the split, then left click once to set it.

Using a Split Screen

When the Word screen has been split, there will be two vertical and horizontal scroll bars, so you can scroll to two different locations in the document. Click inside a part of the upper or lower document to begin typing text or editing.

Split Screen Zooming

The zoom setting for each screen can be changed. For example, all of the pages can be viewed in the upper half of the split screen by reducing the zoom percentage to 25per cent, whereas the lower half could be a larger value for editing text. To do this, click inside the upper split of

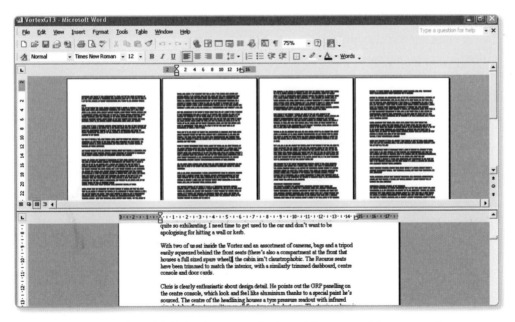

Above: The zoom settings for each half of a split screen can be changed. For instance, all the pages in a document may be seen in the upper half and only one page seen in the lower half.

the document, then alter the zoom setting. Next, click in the lower split of the document and change the zoom setting.

> ## Hot Tip
>
> **Hold down Ctrl+Alt on the keyboard, then press S to switch a split screen on or off.**

Removing a Split Screen

Position the mouse pointer over the dividing line between the two views of the document. When the mouse pointer changes to a cross with double-headed vertical arrows, hold the left button down and drag the dividing line all the way up the screen. Alternatively, click on the Window menu and choose Remove Split (Word pre-2007), or click on the View ribbon tab and select the button labelled Remove Split.

VIEWING MORE THAN ONE WORD DOCUMENT

Two or more Word documents can be viewed on the screen at the same time, which is useful for editing or copying between different documents. Make sure at least two documents are open, then click on the Window menu (Word pre-2007) or the View ribbon tab (Word 2007 and later) and select Arrange All from the menu or ribbon. Each Word document will be displayed in its own window with menu options, toolbar or ribbon buttons and scroll bars. You may want to hide the ribbons or toolbars to create more space.

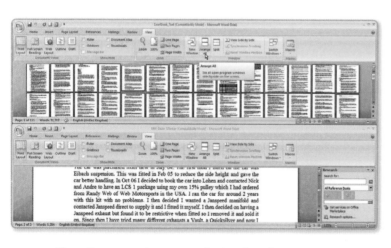

Above: Two or more documents can be viewed together on the screen using Arrange All.

PRINTING

One of the most important aspects of word processing is printing. It's one of the functions of a typewriter, from which the word processor originates. The following pages cover the typical problems that arise with printing and the fastest techniques for effectively printing a document.

PRINT PREVIEW

The best starting point when deciding to print a document is to see what it will look like before the paper starts to churn out of the printer. Whilst the Print Layout view of the document will help, it's best to open the Print Preview screen as a final check. Print Preview can be opened in the following ways:

Hot Tip

Hold down the Ctrl key and press F2 to open the Print Preview screen.

- **Word pre-2007**: Click on the File menu and choose Print Preview, or click on the Print Preview toolbar button on the standard toolbar (it looks like a white piece of paper with a magnifying glass).

- **Word 2007**: Click on the Office button (top-left corner of the screen), move down the menu to Print and across to select Print Preview from the sub-menu.

- **Word 2010**: Click on the File menu and choose Print.

Changing the View in Print Preview

The mouse pointer usually changes to a magnifying glass when the Print Preview screen appears. Left click inside the document to zoom in and out of it (left click several times). There are also other zoom control options on the toolbar or ribbon bar along the top of the screen, plus buttons to choose to view the entire page or multiple pages. These views do not change how the document will be printed.

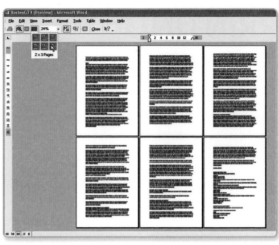

Above: Multiple pages can be displayed on screen

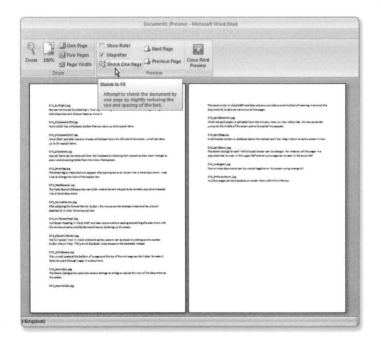

Shrink to One Page

Word can shrink the text in a document to ensure it fits on one page. This should only be done to a document where a few lines of text flow on to a second page, because Word will reduce the size of the font in the document, which can result in the font size being too small to read. In Word 2007 and later versions, the amount of white

Left: The Shrink to Fit or Shrink One Page button in Print Preview tries to reduce the font size and white space to help reduce a document down to one page.

space is also reduced. From within the Print Preview screen, click on the Shrink to Fit or Shrink One Page button.

Above: If Word cannot reduce the font size and white space to make the document fit into one page, a message box will appear.

ADDING HEADERS AND FOOTERS

Headers and footers are useful for displaying information at the top (header) and bottom (footer) of each printed page. Dates, page numbers, document filenames and the name of the author can all be displayed within headers and footers. This information is displayed on the screen and will also be printed.

Inserting a Header or Footer in Word 2007-2010

Click on the Insert ribbon tab and look for the Header and Footer ribbon buttons. Click on one of these buttons and a selection of header styles will appear in a drop-down menu. Choose one of these styles and it will appear in the document. Click inside the areas of the header to add text. Use the ribbon buttons to change the settings and add a date and page numbers. When you have finished, click on the Close Header and Footer button near the top-right corner of the screen.

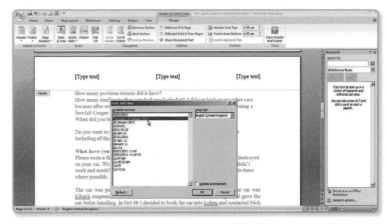

Above: Headers and footers can be added in Word 2007 and later versions via the Insert ribbon tab.

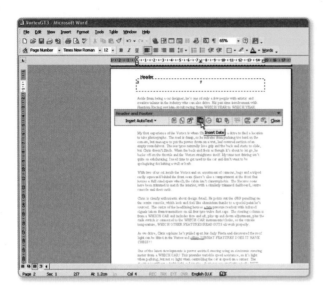

Inserting a Header or Footer in Word Pre-2007

Click on the View menu and choose Header and Footer. A header will appear at the top of the page along with a toolbar. This toolbar can be used to add page numbers, dates and other details. It can also be used to switch between the header and footer and to close, returning to the main text in the document.

Editing a Header or Footer

Make sure the Print Layout view is selected (look at the small buttons in the bottom-left or bottom-right corner of the screen for different view options), so the header/footer can be seen. Double click inside a header or footer to edit it.

Removing Headers and Footers

In Word pre-2007, double click inside the header or footer, then delete its contents. In Word 2007 and later versions, click on the Header or Footer ribbon button in the top-left corner of the screen and a menu will drop down. Choose Remove Header (or Remove Footer) at the bottom of the menu.

TYPICAL PRINTING PROBLEMS

The following section outlines some of the common difficulties experienced when printing Word documents and how to resolve them.

Too Much White Space between the Edge of the Text and the Edge of the Paper

The unused white space between the four edges of the text and the four edges of the paper is known as the margins. These can be altered to help print more or less text on to the paper. In Word pre-2007, click on the File menu and choose Page Setup. In Word 2007 and later versions, click on Page Setup in the Print Preview screen. In all cases, a Page Setup dialogue box will appear. Select the Margins tab and adjust the values for the Top, Bottom, Left and Right margins. Return to Print Preview to see if these changes have helped.

Above: A document's margins can be adjusted to print more or less text on each page.

I Only Want to Print One Page from a Document Containing Lots of Pages

Make sure the cursor is positioned anywhere in the page to be printed, then hold down Ctrl on the keyboard and press P. The Print dialogue box will appear. Under the Page Range section, choose Current Page, then click on OK to proceed with printing.

More Than One Page Is Printed on Each Sheet of Paper

Hold down the Ctrl key on the keyboard and press P to open the Print dialogue box or screen. Look at the bottom-right corner of the dialogue box under the Zoom section and the settings for Pages per sheet. Make sure this is set to 1 page. A setting for more than one page will result in multiple pages being printed on each sheet of paper.

The Print Quality Is Very Poor

Assuming there are no problems with the printer (such as low ink levels or blocked jets), there is a draft-quality print setting in Word 2003 and earlier versions. To check this isn't switched on, press Ctrl+P on the keyboard to open the Print dialogue box, then click on the Options button near the bottom-left corner of the screen. A second dialogue box will appear. Look at the Printing options in the top-left corner of the box and make sure there isn't a tick mark against Draft output.

IMPROVING A DOCUMENT

CREATING A DOCUMENT STRUCTURE

A structurally organized document is easier to understand and manage and looks consistently professional in its presentation. The following pages outline some of the useful tools in Word that can help create a structure and use it to create a contents page.

HEADINGS

The use of headings throughout a document allows Word to understand how it is structured, whether it's a report with a few headings and sub-headings or a reference book with chapters, headings and several layers of sub-headings. Word's headings use a number order system, with Heading 1 being at the top (for example, a chapter heading), followed by Heading 2, Heading 3 and so on. It is best to structure a document according to this heading hierarchy.

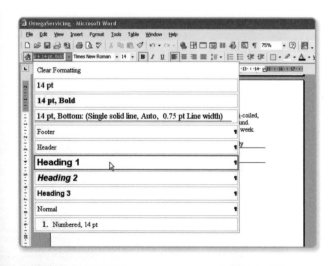

Applying a Heading

Position the cursor inside the text that will be used as a heading. In Word pre-2007, the Formatting toolbar has a style drop-down menu, which lists all of the available headings. Open this drop-down list and select a heading from it. In Word 2007 and later versions, click on the Home ribbon tab and a series of

Left: Headings in Word pre-2007 can be selected from the Styles drop-down list on the Formatting toolbar.

headings will be displayed across the top of the screen (there is a scroll bar to the right which shows more heading options).

Modifying a Heading

The font, size and colour used in a heading in some cases won't match the rest of the text in the document, but fortunately, these attributes can be changed via a dialogue box. This dialogue box is opened in different ways, depending on the version of Word. The following list explains the different methods:

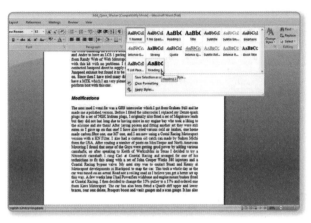

Above: The different headings can be found in Word 2007 and later versions on the Home ribbon tab.

→ **Word 2000 and earlier:** Click on the Format menu and choose Style. From the dialogue box that appears, select the heading you want to change and click on the Modify button.

Hot Tip

Select some text to which to apply a heading, then hold down the Ctrl and Alt keys and press 1 to apply Heading 1, 2 to apply Heading 2 and 3 to apply Heading 3.

→ **Word 2002–2003:** Click on the Format menu and choose Styles and Formatting. A long list will appear down the right-hand side of the screen. Position the mouse over the heading to modify, click on the drop-down triangle to the right of it and select Modify from the menu that appears.

→ **Word 2007 and later:** Hold down the Ctrl+Shift+Alt keys on the keyboard, then press the letter S. A list of styles, including headings, will appear. Position the mouse pointer over the one to edit, then click on the drop-down triangle to the right of it and choose Modify.

Above: The font, size and colour applied to a heading can be modified.

Changing the Font, Size and Colour of a Heading

After choosing to modify a heading (see the previous section), there may be some font options displayed inside a dialogue box. Otherwise, click on the Format button and a menu will appear with more options for modifying the heading. Choose one of the options and another dialogue box will open to allow changes to be made to the heading.

Adding More Headings

More headings are available, but are often not displayed. In Word 2007 and later versions, the next heading number is automatically displayed once the last heading number has been used. In 2002–2003, click on the drop-down triangle in the bottom-right corner of the Styles and Formatting task pane to see All styles (all the heading numbers will be listed). In Word 2000 and earlier versions, click on the Format menu and choose Style. From the dialogue box that appears, choose All styles from the List section, select a style and click on Apply.

Hot Tip

Headings can be found in Word 2002–2003 by opening the Styles and Formatting task pane on the right-hand side of the screen. This can be opened by clicking on the button on the far left of the Formatting toolbar, which looks like two letter A's.

INSERTING PAGE NUMBERS

Page numbers can be displayed throughout a document. Click on the Insert menu or ribbon tab and choose the Page Numbers option or button. A dialogue box or drop-down menu will appear with a number of choices for the

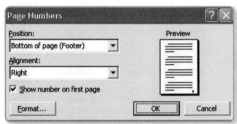

Above: Click on the Insert menu and choose Page Numbers in Word pre-2007 to see the dialogue box shown here. Then choose where to add the page numbers and click on OK.

position of the page numbers and whether the first page should show a page number (it can be omitted if the first page is a front cover).

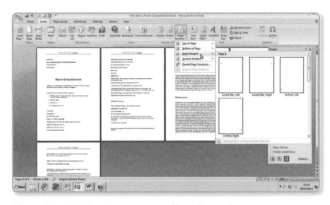

Above: Word 2007 and later versions offer a choice of page number styles and positions on the Insert ribbon tab.

CREATING A TABLE OF CONTENTS

Word can instantly create a table of contents for a document, but the document must contain Headings (Heading 1, Heading 2, Heading 3), which are used within the contents page and referred to by page number. If a document contains Headings, the following instructions explain how to insert a table of contents into the document.

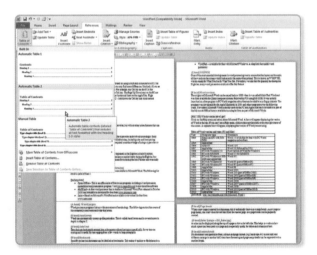

Above: A table of contents can be quickly created in Word 2007 and later versions. A drop-down menu on the References ribbon tab gives a choice of styles.

Creating a Contents Page in Word 2007-2010

Position the cursor at the point where the contents page needs to be created. Click on the References ribbon tab, then select the Table of Contents button in the top-left corner of the screen. A sample list of contents-page styles will appear. Choose one from the list and a table of contents will be created in the document. Each heading (Heading 1, Heading 2, Heading 3) will be listed alongside its relevant page number.

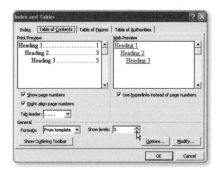

Above: An Index and Tables dialogue box is used in Word pre-2007 to set up and create a table of contents.

Creating a Contents Page in Word Pre-2007

Position the cursor at the point where the contents page needs to be created. Click on the Insert menu and choose Index and Tables, or select Reference and, from the sub-menu that appears, click on Index and Tables. An Index and Tables dialogue box will appear. Select the Table of Contents tab. There are a number of settings in this dialogue box, including the heading levels (Heading 1, Heading 2, Heading 3), which may need adjusting in the Show levels section. There are also tick boxes for page numbers and alignment. Click on OK to create the table of contents in the document.

Jumping to Pages via the Table of Contents

Position the mouse pointer over a heading in the table of contents and hold down the Ctrl key on the keyboard. The mouse pointer will change to a hand symbol. With the Ctrl key still held down on the keyboard, left click on the heading and Word will jump to that heading within the document.

Updating a Table of Contents

If headings are changed or moved within a document, or new ones created, then the table of contents will need to be updated. Right click inside the table of contents and choose Update Field from the shortcut menu that appears. A small box will appear asking whether to update the entire table or just the page numbers. Choose one of the options and click on OK.

Deleting a Table of Contents

The quickest way to delete a table of contents is to select it and press Delete on the keyboard. Selecting a table of contents can be a little awkward. Starting at the top of the table of contents, hold the left button down on the mouse and move the mouse pointer down and across the items listed in the table of contents. If only part of the table of contents is selected, it can still be deleted, then the remainder selected and deleted.

PRE-SET ATTRIBUTES

Word has a selection of pre-set fonts, colours and sizes that can be applied throughout a document to make it look professional and save time having to choose the correct ones. These are known as themes or style sets.

THEMES IN WORD PRE-2007

The fonts, colours, sizes and other attributes used throughout a document can be presented professionally and consistently with a theme. There are a number of themes already stored in Word that enable headings, lists, lines and main text to be displayed in specific colours and sizes. To see and apply the themes available in Word pre-2007, click on the Format menu and choose Theme. From the dialogue box that appears, select from the list on the left and see a sample of it on the right. Click on OK to apply that theme.

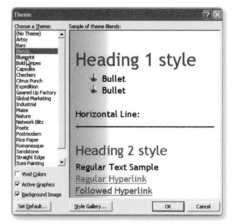

Above: Word pre-2007 can use themes to apply pre-set colours, fonts, sizes and other attributes to a document.

STYLE SETS IN WORD 2007-2010

Word 2007 and later versions uses style sets to apply pre-set colours, fonts and sizes to headings and text in a document. The different style sets can be quickly seen by clicking on the Home ribbon tab, selecting the Change Styles button near the top-right corner of the screen and choosing Style Set. A sub-menu will appear with a list of pre-set styles. Hover the mouse over them and the text in the document will change to that particular style set. Click on a style to apply it.

ORGANIZING TEXT

Text in a Word document is often easier to read and understand when it is presented in a format other than lines and lines of text. The following section shows how to create bulleted and numbered lists, arrange text into a table, split sections of text with lines and display text in multiple columns.

BULLETED AND NUMBERED LISTS

Word can display lists of text with a range of different bullets or styles of sequential numbers or letters. A bullet point or number can be quickly added to a line or paragraph of text by clicking on the appropriate button on the Formatting toolbar in Word 2003 and earlier versions, or the Home ribbon tab in Word 2007 and later versions. Word will add a number or a bullet, depending on which toolbar button was selected. Upon pressing return, Word will create the next number or the same bullet on a new line, allowing the next point in the list to be created.

Hot Tip

Start a line of text with the number 1 or an asterisk (*), add a couple of spaces, then type some text and press Return. Word will automatically start a numbered list or convert the asterisk into a bullet point.

Switching off a Bulleted or Numbered List

When you have finished creating a bulleted or numbered list, press Return (also known as the Enter key) twice on the keyboard. The cursor will move down two lines and stop adding a bullet or number to the beginning of each line.

Changing the Type of Numbers or Bullets (Word 2007 and Later Versions)

Make sure the cursor is positioned inside the text of the bulleted or numbered list. Click on the Home ribbon tab and look for the toolbar buttons at the top of the screen for creating a bulleted or numbered list. Each button has a drop-down arrow next to it. Click on the drop-

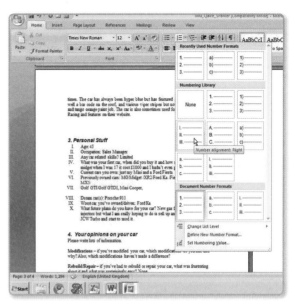

down arrow and a palette of bullet or number styles will appear. Choose one of these and all the bullet points or numbers will be changed.

Above: Word 2007 and later versions offer a choice of bullet or number styles to apply to a list.

Changing the Type of Numbers or Bullets (Word Pre-2007)

Right click on the text inside a bulleted or numbered list and choose Bullets and Numbers from the shortcut menu that appears. A Bullets and Numbering dialogue box will appear. Select the Bulleted or Numbered tab, then choose a style. Click on OK to apply that style to the list.

Multi-Level Bullets and Numbers

A bulleted or numbered list can have sub-points or sub-levels. This is useful for breaking down points in a list. When writing

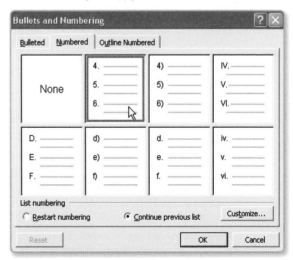

Above: Word pre-2007 uses a dialogue box to change the style of bullet points or numbers.

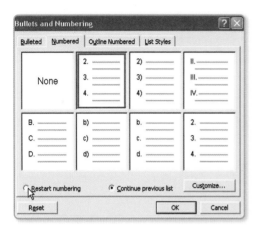

Above: If the values in a numbered list are incorrect in Word pre-2007, use the Restart numbering option in the Bullets and Numbering dialogue box to rectify.

Above: Problems with numbered lists can sometimes be rectified in Word 2007 and later versions using the Set Numbering Value dialogue box.

a bulleted or numbered list, a sub-point can be created using a new bullet or number by pressing the Tab key on the keyboard. The bullet or number will move to the right and change to a different style (for example, 2.1). An existing bullet point or number point can be converted into a sub-level by positioning the cursor at the beginning of the line of text and pressing the Tab key on the keyboard.

Adding and Removing Levels

Several levels of bullets or numbers can be added to a list. Press the Tab key to move down a level, or hold down the Shift key and press the Tab key to move back up a level. Make sure the cursor is next to the bullet or number and at the beginning of the line of text before pressing the Tab key or Shift+Tab. If it's within the text, pressing the Tab key will move the text instead.

Changing the Level Style

The style of levels used in a bulleted or numbered list can be changed using the same technique for changing the type of numbers or bullets mentioned earlier. *See* Changing the Type of Numbers or Bullets (pages 96 and 97).

Numbered List Trouble

Sometimes, the sequence of numbers in a list is incorrect. The numbers may continue from a previous list or start again at 1. This can be easily resolved by right clicking inside the text where the number is wrong. In Word 2007 and later versions, position the mouse pointer over Numbering, then select Set Numbering Value from the sub-menu. In Word pre-2007, right click in the same manner, but choose Bullets and Numbering. In both cases, a dialogue box will appear with choices for restarting numbers, continuing from a previous list and setting a number at which to start.

TABLES

Complicated text can be easier to understand when displayed in a table. Word allows tables to be copied from other programs or created within a document and even drawn on the screen. Before creating a table, however, there is some jargon that is worth knowing:

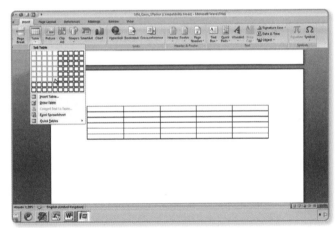

Cell: An individual box inside a table, which can be used to display text and images.

Row: A line of cells across a table.

Column: A line of cells down a table.

Inserting a Table in Word 2007 and Later Versions

Above: Word 2007 and later versions use the Table button on the Insert ribbon tab from which you can choose the number of rows and columns for a table.

Click on the Insert menu or ribbon tab, then select the Table button near the top-left corner of the screen. A grid pattern will appear below this button. Move the mouse pointer down and across this grid to choose the number of rows and columns for the table. The table will be automatically displayed in the document. Left click to complete choosing the number of rows and columns.

Above: Click on the Table menu in Word pre-2007, choose Insert and select Table to display this dialogue box. Choose the number of rows and columns for the table, then click on OK.

Hot Tip

When drawing a table, Word will adjust the lines for the rows and columns to make sure they are straight, so you don't need to have a steady hand when drawing them.

Inserting a Table in Word Pre-2007

Click on the Table menu, choose Insert and select Table from the sub-menu. An Insert Table dialogue box will appear. Alter the values for the number of rows and columns to use in the table, then click on OK to close the dialogue box and create the table in the document.

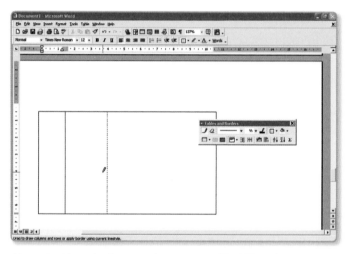

Above: A table can be drawn in a document using Word 97 or a later version. First, draw a box, then draw the lines for the rows and columns.

Drawing a Table in Word 97 and Later Versions

A table can be drawn on the screen in Word 97 and later versions. In Word pre-2007, click on the Table menu and choose Draw Table. In Word 2007 and later versions, click on the Insert ribbon tab, select the Table button and choose Draw Table. In all cases, the mouse pointer will change to a pencil. First, draw a box inside the document, then draw the lines for the rows and columns. If an unwanted line is drawn, click on the eraser button, then draw over it to remove it. Click on the Draw Table button to continue drawing lines.

Adding a Table to Existing Text

If some text already exists in a document and you want to display it in a table, then the following methods can be used:

- **Select the text to be displayed in the table, then follow the instructions on inserting a table.**

- **Draw a table around the text.**

- **Create an empty table, then cut and paste the text into it.**

Adding a table to existing text can sometimes be awkward and in many cases one of the above solutions will work while the others may incorrectly rearrange the text, so be prepared to undo an action if it goes wrong (press Ctrl and Z on the keyboard).

Adding More Rows and Columns

Right click inside the table and if an option to insert more rows or columns is displayed, choose one of these. Otherwise, move the mouse pointer to the left of the table and right click to insert another row, or move the mouse pointer above the table and right click to insert another column.

Deleting Rows, Columns and Tables

Rows and columns can be deleted in the same way they are inserted. Right click inside the table, right click to the left of the

Hot Tip

Another row can be quickly added to a table by positioning the cursor outside the table, on the right side. When the cursor is in this position, press Return and another row will be inserted.

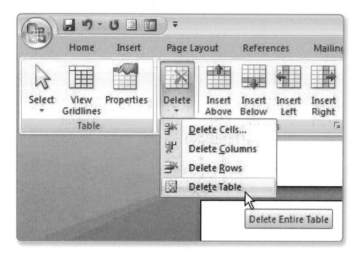

row to be deleted or right click above the column to delete. Choose one of the options from the shortcut menu to delete a row or column. An entire table can be deleted by positioning the cursor inside it, then either clicking on the Table menu, choosing Delete and selecting Table from the sub-menu (Word pre-2007), or selecting the Layout ribbon tab (Word 2007–2010), clicking on the Delete button and choosing Delete Table.

Above: A table can be deleted in Word 2007 and later versions by positioning the cursor inside it, then clicking on the Layout ribbon tab, selecting the Delete button and choosing Delete Table.

Adjusting Column Widths and Row Heights

Position the mouse pointer over a line that divides two columns or rows inside a table. When the mouse pointer changes to a cross with double-headed arrows, hold the left button down and move the mouse to resize the width of the columns or height of the rows.

Alternatively, the width of every column or height of every row can all be adjusted to the same dimensions. Click on the Table menu in Word pre-2007 (make sure the cursor is inside the table), choose AutoFit and select Distribute Rows Evenly, or Distribute Columns Evenly. In Word 2007–2010, click on the Layout ribbon tab and use the Distribute Rows or Distribute Columns buttons near the top of the screen.

SEPARATING SECTIONS WITH LINES

Flowing text can be separated within a document using a line or double line across the full width of the page. This is known as a border and is covered in more detail under Adding

Colour (*see* page 110). The fastest method of adding a line across the page is as follows:

-  **Three *****: Type three asterisks at the beginning of a line, press Return and they will be converted into a thick dotted line. Press delete or backspace to remove the line.

- **Three ===**: Type three equal symbols at the beginning of a line and they will be converted into a double line after pressing Return.

- **Three ——-**: Type three minus symbols at the beginning of a line and they will be converted into a single line after pressing Return.

COLUMNS OF TEXT

Text is usually displayed on the page of a Word document in one column, but several columns can be used instead. Existing text can be displayed in multiple columns or the columns can be set before typing the text. Select the existing text to be converted to columns or position the cursor at the point where new text will be displayed in multiple columns. The following points explain how to apply multiple columns according to the version of Word in use:

→ **Word pre-2007**: Click on the Format menu and choose Columns. From the dialogue box that appears, select the number of columns to use then click on OK.

→ **Word 2007–2010**: Click on the Page Layout ribbon tab and select the Columns button near the top left of the screen. Choose one of the options for the number of columns or select More Columns and a dialogue box will appear with further choices.

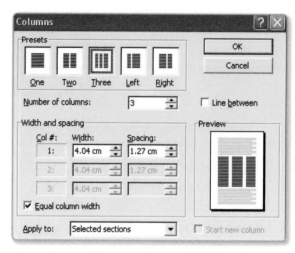

Above: Word pre-2007 uses a dialogue box to specify the number of columns to be used on a page.

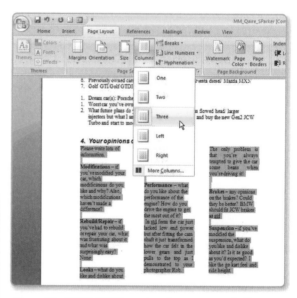

Above: Word 2007–2010 has a drop-down menu on the Page Layout ribbon tab to enable text to be converted to columns.

Hot Tip

Word pre-2007 has a button on the standard toolbar that looks like two columns. Click on this and select the number of columns to apply.

SORTING A LIST OR COLUMN IN A TABLE

Text in a bulleted list, table or simply displayed on several lines can be sorted numerically or alphabetically. This can save hours of moving text to different positions in the document.

Sorting a List or Lines of Text

Select the lines of text that need to be sorted. In Word pre-2007, click on the Table menu and choose Sort. In later versions, click on the Home ribbon tab and select the Sort button in the top middle of the screen (it has the letters A and Z displayed on it with an arrow pointing downwards). A Sort Text dialogue box will appear. If necessary, change the settings to specify ascending or descending and whether the words that need to be sorted are text, dates or numbers. Click on OK and the selected text will be sorted.

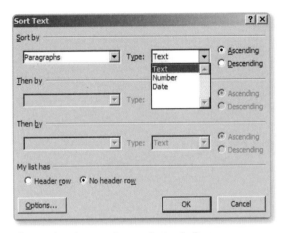

Above: A list of text can be sorted using the Sort Text dialogue box.

Sorting a Column in a Table

Position the cursor inside the table. In Word pre-2007, click on the Table menu and choose Sort. In later versions of Word, click on the Home ribbon tab and select the Sort button (it has the letters A and Z displayed on it with an arrow pointing downwards). In all cases a Sort dialogue box will appear. Make sure the correct column is chosen and if the table has headings across the top, select the Header row option to prevent them being sorted. Choose the type of data that will be sorted (number, text or date) and the sort order (ascending or descending), then click on OK.

ADDING IMAGES

Pictures, drawings, company logos and photographs can all be inserted into a Word document to help illustrate reports, newsletters and letterheads. The following section shows where images can be found, how to insert your own images and how to change the size and position of them.

CLIP ART

Pre-made drawings and images are known as Clip Art. These are available through Microsoft Word, other programs and on the Internet. Each piece of Clip Art is a file with a filename and an extension such as JPG, TIF and BMP.

Clip Art Library

Word uses Microsoft Office's Clip Art library, which contains an assortment of illustrations. These can be accessed in Word 2003 and earlier versions by clicking on the Insert menu, choosing Picture and selecting Clip Art from the sub-menu. Either a dialogue box will appear or a Clip Art task pane on the right side (Word 2002–2003). In Word 2007–2010, click on the Insert ribbon tab and select the Clip Art button. A Clip Art task pane will appear on the right side of the screen.

Searching for Clip Art

The Clip Art dialogue box or task pane can be used to search for types of Clip Art (for example, money) by typing in a keyword in

Left: The Clip Art dialogue box or task pane can be used to search for a wide range of images that can be inserted into a document.

the search box. Word will display any relevant Clip Art it finds according to keyword(s) entered. To add some Clip Art to a document, select the image and it will be inserted where the cursor was positioned. In some cases, you may need to double click on it, click on Insert or drag and drop it into the document. The Clip Art can then be resized and moved, just like a drawing shape.

LOGOS, PHOTOS AND COMMERCIAL IMAGES

Images that are not listed in the Clip Art library can be inserted. In Word pre-2007, click on the Insert menu, choose Picture and Select From File. In Word 2007–2010, click on the Insert ribbon tab and select the button labelled Picture (near the top-left corner of the screen). In all cases, an Insert Picture dialogue box will appear, which is similar to the dialogue box for opening a Word document. Locate a picture, then click on the Insert button. The picture will be added as an object to the document and can be resized and moved, just like a drawing shape.

WORDART

WordArt can help produce a professional-looking title in a newsletter, report or similar document. To add a piece of WordArt, click on the Insert menu, choose Picture and select WordArt from the

Above: Photos, drawings and other illustrations can be inserted into a Word document.

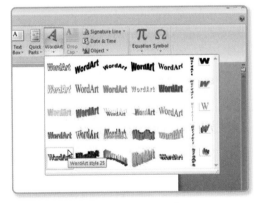

Above: WordArt can be inserted in Word 2007–2010 by clicking on the Insert ribbon tab and selecting the WordArt button.

sub-menu, or click on the Insert ribbon tab (Word 2007–2010) and click on the WordArt button. In both cases, a palette of WordArt styles will appear in a dialogue box or drop-down menu. Choose a WordArt style (and click on OK in Word pre-2007), then type the text for the WordArt title and click on OK.

RESIZING, MOVING AND DELETING IMAGES

Photos, drawings, WordArt and other similar illustrations can be moved to different locations in a document, resized and deleted.

Above: WordArt and images can be resized by selecting the object, then hovering the mouse pointer over the dots around it. When the mouse pointer changes to a double-headed arrow, hold the left button down and move the mouse to resize the object.

Resizing WordArt and Images

Click inside the object to select it. A box and a series of dots will appear around it. Position the mouse pointer over any of the dots around the object. When the mouse pointer changes to a double-headed arrow, hold the left button down and move the mouse to resize the object.

Moving WordArt and Images

WordArt and images are objects that fit on a line between the text in a document. So if the WordArt or image has to be moved, it has to be moved to another line in the document. If a document contains no text, the WordArt or image can be moved down the document by positioning the cursor before it, then pressing Return on the keyboard (press Delete to move it up the document). If a document contains text, the WordArt or image can be dragged and dropped to a different location (position the mouse pointer over the object, hold the left button down and move to another location in the document, then release the left button).

ADDING COLOUR

A document can be easily changed from the standard, plain white background by adding colours, borders and images. The following section shows how to change the background colour, choose a page border and insert a watermark.

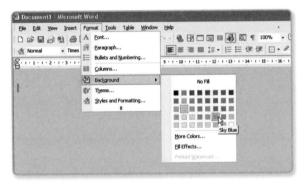

Above: The background colour can be changed in Word pre-2007 by clicking on the Format menu.

CHANGING THE BACKGROUND COLOUR IN WORD PRE-2007

Click on the Format menu, choose Background and a palette of colours will appear on a sub-menu. Choose a colour from here, or select More Colors or Fill Effects for further choices.

CHANGING THE PAGE COLOUR IN WORD 2007–2010

Click on the Page Layout ribbon tab and select the Page Color button. A palette of colours will drop down and the colour of the document will change to whatever colour the mouse pointer is positioned over. Select More Colors or Fill Effects for further choices, or select a colour from the palette.

Hot Tip

Avoid using a background colour that clashes with the font colour (for example, a dark blue background with a black font), unless you also intend to change the font colour.

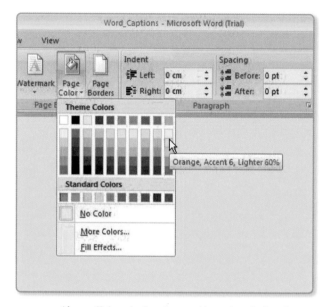

Above: Click on the Page Layout ribbon tab and select the Page Color button to choose a colour for the document.

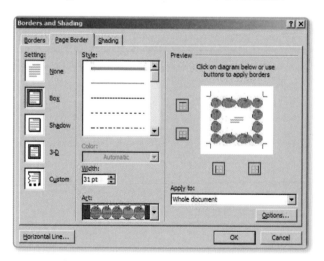

Above: A border can be added to every page in a document. Styles range from lines and dots to artwork.

Switching off a Page or Background Colour

Click on the Format menu in Word pre-2007, choose Background and select No Fill. In Word 2007–2010, click on the Page Layout ribbon tab, select the Page Color button and choose No Color from the palette.

PAGE BORDERS

A border can be added to each page in a document with various style options for colours, 3-D and thickness. To create a page border, click on the Format menu in Word pre-2007 and select Borders and Shading. In Word 2007–2010, click on the Page Layout ribbon tab and select the Page Borders button. In both cases, a Borders and Shading dialogue box will appear. Select the Page Border tab, then

Hot Tip
A page border can be removed by returning to the Borders and Shading dialogue box and selecting None in the top-left corner of the box.

choose a type of border, a style, colour and width. Click on OK to return to the document and see the border (you may need to switch to Print Layout view to see it).

ADDING A BORDER TO A PARAGRAPH

Select the paragraph or block of text to which you want to add a border, then click on the Format menu in Word pre-2007 and select Borders and Shading, or click on the Page Layout ribbon tab in Word 2007–2010 and select the Page Borders button. The Borders and Shading dialogue box will appear. Make sure the Borders tab is selected, then choose a type of border, style, colour and width. Click on OK to return to the document and see the border around the selected text.

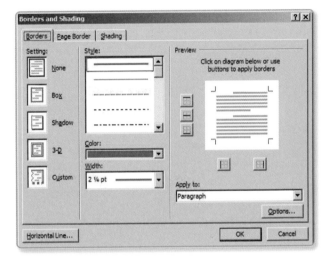

Above: A paragraph of text in a document can stand out by adding a border to it.

WATERMARKS

A watermark is useful for printed and protected documents (such as a PDF) for quotations, legal correspondence or helping to indicate a document is a draft or final copy. The watermark is a faint piece of text or an image that's displayed across each page.

Inserting a Watermark in Word 2007-2010

Click on the Page Layout ribbon tab and select the Watermark button. A palette of watermark styles with text will appear. If one of these can be used, select it. Otherwise, click on Custom Watermark and a Printed Watermark dialogue box will appear. If an image will be used for the watermark (for example, a company logo), select Picture watermark and then click on the Select

Left: A watermark can be quickly added to a document in Word 2007–2010 by clicking on the Page Layout ribbon tab and selecting the Watermark button.

Picture button to find a suitable image. If text will form the watermark, select this option, then enter the text to display and choose a font, size, colour and layout. Click on OK to insert the watermark.

Inserting a Watermark in Word 2002–2003

Click on the Format menu, choose Background and select Printed Watermark from the sub-menu. A Printed Watermark dialogue box will appear. If an image will be used for the watermark (for example, a company logo), select Picture watermark and then click on the Select Picture button to find a suitable image. If text will form the watermark, select this option, then enter the text to display and choose a font, size, colour and layout. Click on OK to insert the watermark.

Removing a Watermark

In Word 2007–2010, click on the Watermark button on the Page Layout ribbon tab and select Remove Watermark from the bottom of the menu. In Word 2002–2003, return to the Printed Watermark dialogue box and select the option at the top, No Watermark, then click on OK.

Left: The Printed Watermark dialogue box allows a custom watermark to be created and added to a document.

ADDING INFORMATION

Information can be presented in a variety of formats in a Word document, including a chart, process flow diagram and organizational chart. The following pages show how to create these features and include them in a Word document.

CHARTS

Pie charts, bar charts, column charts and a wide assortment of other charts can be created in Word and displayed in a document. The data used in a chart can be entered in Word and edited, and the chart can be customized.

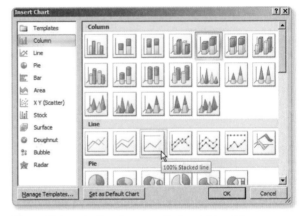

Above: Click on the Chart button on the Insert ribbon tab in Word 2007–2010 to see a choice of chart types.

Creating a Chart in Word 2007-2010

Click on the Insert ribbon tab and select the Chart button. An Insert Chart dialogue box will appear with a choice of charts. Choose one from here, then click on OK. A chart will appear in the document with a screen from Microsoft Excel alongside or near it. The Excel screen displays the data for the chart. All the headings, titles and data used in the chart can be changed using the Excel screen. After editing this information, click on the red X-button in the top-right corner of the Excel screen to close it.

Editing a Chart in Word 2007-2010

Click inside the chart to select it and a Chart Tools ribbon will appear along the top of the screen with ribbon tabs for Design, Layout and Format. Click on these tabs to see a range of buttons that will help to edit the chart. Specific objects inside the chart (for example, the gridlines or a column) can be changed by right clicking on them and choosing Format from the shortcut menu (the wording may be different, depending on what object has been right clicked on).

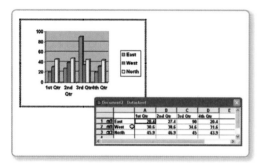

Above: When a chart is inserted in Word pre-2007, a standard chart appears with data displayed in a grid. This data can be changed to in turn change the chart.

Creating a Chart in Word Pre-2007

Click on the Insert menu, choose Picture and select Chart from the sub-menu. A standard chart will appear on screen with the data displayed in a grid – the grid isn't permanently displayed in the document. The data, headings and titles used in the chart can all be changed by changing the information in the grid. Click elsewhere in the document to finish editing the chart – the chart will remain in the document but the grid will disappear. The grid can be reopened by double clicking on the chart.

Editing a Chart in Word Pre-2007

Double click inside the chart to start editing it. The grid containing the data used in the chart will appear. A Chart menu will also appear. Click on the Chart menu and choose Chart Type to change the style of chart. Right click on parts of the chart and choose Format (the wording may be different, depending on what object is clicked on) to change colours, fonts and other attributes.

ORGANIZATION CHART

An organization chart helps to illustrate the structure of people in a business, a system in the workplace or even the pages of a website. Microsoft's organization chart is an additional feature for Word and other programs. It allows a structure of boxes to be created with text in

Hot Tip

A chart can be removed from a document by clicking on the edge of it to select it, then pressing Delete on the keyboard.

each box. The layout of the organization chart can be amended and boxes can be added and removed.

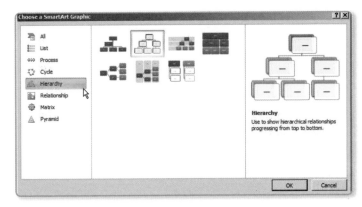

Above: Organization charts and similar styles of diagrams can be inserted in Word 2007–2010 by clicking on the Insert ribbon tab and selecting the SmartArt button.

Creating an Organization Chart in Word 2007-2010

Click on the Insert ribbon tab and select the SmartArt button. A dialogue box will appear with a wide range of diagrams.

The styles of diagrams are listed on the left, with samples from each style on the right. Choose one, then click on OK to insert it into the Word document. The text inside the chart can be changed by clicking on it, then using the small box to type new text. There are also a number of buttons across the top of the screen, which can be used to change the diagram (click on the Design and the Format ribbon tabs).

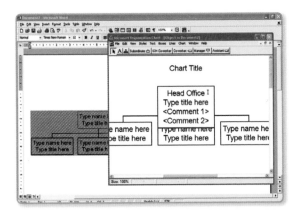

Above: In Word 2000 and earlier versions, an organization chart is created in a separate box with its own toolbar buttons.

Creating an Organization Chart in Word Pre-2007

In Word 2002–2003, click on the Insert menu, choose Picture and select Organization Chart. In earlier versions of Word, click on the Insert menu and choose Object for a dialogue box to appear – scroll down to select MS Organization Chart, then click on OK. In all cases, an organization chart will appear on screen and can be changed by clicking inside the boxes and overtyping the text. There are also toolbar buttons to change the structure of the chart and add more boxes.

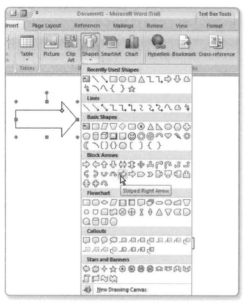

Above: Block arrows can be used to create a process flow diagram. These can be found in Word 2007–2010 on the Insert ribbon tab, under Shapes.

Hot Tip

A box in an organization chart can be removed by clicking on the edge of it and pressing Delete on the keyboard. If the cursor is inside the box, it cannot be deleted.

PROCESS FLOW DIAGRAMS

A process flow diagram can be created in Word to help illustrate step-by-step instructions and procedures. Drawing objects such as block arrows, boxes and circles can be used to create these process flow diagrams. In Word pre-2007, block arrows and similar shapes are on the AutoShapes button of the Drawing toolbar. The Drawing toolbar is usually displayed along the bottom of the screen. In Word 2007–2010, click on the Insert ribbon tab and select the Shapes button for a palette of shapes, including block arrows.

Adding Text to a Block Arrow or Box

Text can be added to most drawn objects, such as an arrow, box or circle. Right click on the drawn object and select Add Text. Type the text inside the object, then click away from he object to finish.

Hot Tip

The Drawing toolbar can be quickly displayed in Word pre-2007 by right clicking on any toolbar button and selecting Drawing from the shortcut menu that appears.

Right: A drawn object can be resized by selecting it and positioning the mouse pointer over the dots or squares around it. Hold the left button down on the mouse and move the mouse pointer to resize the drawn object.

Resizing Drawn Objects

A drawn object can be resized by selecting it, then hovering the mouse pointer over any of the small squares or circles around it. When the mouse pointer changes to a double-headed arrow, hold the left button down and move the mouse to resize the object.

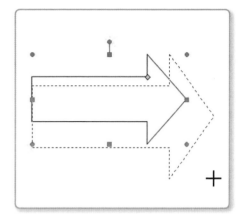

Rotating a Drawn Object

In Word 2000 and earlier versions, select an object and click on the Rotate button (looks like an arrow in the shape of a circle) on the Drawing toolbar. A series of green circles will appear around the object. In later versions of Word, one green circle will appear above the object after selecting it. In all cases, position the mouse pointer over a/the green circle and when it changes to an arrow in the shape of a circle, hold the left button down and move the mouse to rotate the object.

Grouping Objects for a Process Flow Diagram

A process flow diagram consisting of several shapes can be difficult to move around the screen. However, if all the shapes are grouped together, they can be easily moved together. To group shapes together, select one shape, then hold the Shift key down on the

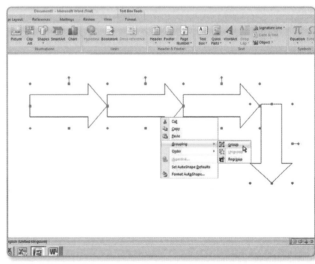

Right: Several drawn objects can be grouped by selecting them, then right clicking and choosing Grouping, followed by Group from the sub-menu.

> ## Hot Tip
>
> **Use Connectors to link between shapes. These lines automatically connect or snap to shapes, making it easier to draw process flow diagrams.**

keyboard and continue to select all the other shapes. Once they have all been selected, right click on one of them, choose Group or Grouping and select Group from the sub-menu. Try moving one of the shapes and all of them will move. To ungroup the shapes, right click on a shape, choose Group or Grouping and select Ungroup from the sub-menu.

USING DATA FROM OTHER PROGRAMS

Charts, tables, illustrations and other information can be included in a Word document. There are various methods for inserting this type of data or objects, depending on how they were created and which program was used.

Inserting Programs and Files

If a slide from a PowerPoint presentation, worksheet from an Excel workbook or pages from a PDF need to be included in a Word document, there are a few methods available. Click on the Insert menu or ribbon tab and choose Object. From the dialogue box that appears, select the Create from File tab and click on the Browse button to locate a specific file and insert the contents of it into the Word document. This will allow the inserted file to be edited using its original program, but sometimes only the first page of the file is inserted.

Left: The contents of a non-Word file can be inserted into a document as an object. However, sometimes only the first page of a file is inserted.

Copy, Paste Special

Copying information from a program and pasting it into a Word document is often successful. After copying the information, select a point in the Word document to place it, then right click and choose Paste. The pasted information may have to be resized.

However, if this method is not successful, try using Paste Special instead. In Word 2007–2010, select the Home ribbon tab, click on the drop-down arrow below the Paste button and choose Paste Special. In earlier versions of Word, click on the Edit menu and choose Paste Special. In all cases, a dialogue box will appear with choices for how to paste the information into Word.

Taking a Screen Shot

Most keyboards have a Print Screen button, which takes a copy of whatever is on the screen. This is useful for copying the contents of a file and pasting them into a Word document. After taking a screen shot from another program, position the mouse pointer inside the document where this information can be used, then right click and choose Paste. The copied information will usually be pasted as an image, which can be moved and resized. If this isn't successful, see the previous section on using Paste Special.

Screenshots in Word 2007-2010

Word 2007–2010 has a screen shot feature which can copy the screen from any program that is open and not minimized to the Taskbar. Click on the Insert ribbon tab and choose Screenshot. A palette of screenshots from all the open programs will be displayed. Select one of them to paste it into the Word document.

Above: Screenshots are available on the Insert ribbon tab in Word 2007–2010.

TIME SAVERS & TROUBLESHOOTING

TIME SAVERS AS YOU TYPE

There are several tools and keyboard shortcuts that can help with typing text more efficiently and correct mistakes when they occur. The following section shows how to use Word's AutoCorrect and AutoText tools and customize them to your needs.

WRONG CASE

Press the Caps Lock by accident and there's nothing worse than seeing several words or lines of text all in upper case across the screen. Fortunately, you don't have to delete the text and start again. Instead, just select all of the text that is displayed in upper case, then hold the Shift key down on the keyboard and press F3. The text will change to lower case and if you press F3 again (with the shift key still held down), it will change again and eventually change back to upper case.

THe|

The

Above: Hold the Shift key down for too long when typing a capital letter and THe will be typed with two upper case letters. Luckily, Word will automatically correct this mistake.

TWO CAPITALS

If you hold the Shift key down on the keyboard when typing a capital letter, it's easy to hold it down for too long and the first two letters of a word will be displayed as capitals (for example, THe). If this happens, Word will automatically correct this mistake and change the second capital letter in the word to a lower case letter. This is known as AutoCorrect and is covered in more detail in this chapter.

CAPS LOCK OFF/ON

Sometimes, the Caps Lock can be accidentally switched on, so when the Shift key is held down to type a capital letter, Word produces a lower case letter instead. Consequently, a whole word could look back to front with a lower case letter at the start and upper case letters for the rest of the word. Luckily, Word can recognize this mistake and will not only swap the case of the word so that it starts with a capital letter, but it will also switch off Caps Lock on the keyboard!

AUTOMATIC SPELLING CORRECTION

Word can automatically correct a number of typical spelling mistakes. For example, type the word 'thier' and it will be automatically corrected to 'their' after pressing the space-bar or Return. This is known as AutoCorrect.

I DON'T WANT TO AUTOCORRECT A MISTAKE

If a spelling mistake or misuse of capitals is automatically corrected by Word, but you don't want it correcting, then there are some quick solutions, depending on the version of Word you are using:

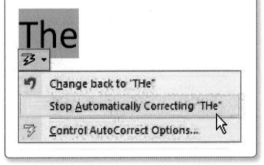

Above: If Word 2007–2010 automatically corrects a spelling mistake or misuse of capitals but you don't want it correcting, click on the Smart Tag for some methods of reversing the correction.

➔ **Word 2007–2010**: Hover the mouse pointer over the corrected word and a small blue line will appear underneath the word. Move the mouse pointer over the line and a Smart Tag will appear. Click on this tag and a menu will drop down with some options for reversing the correction.

➔ **Word pre-2007**: Continue typing, then return to the corrected word, change it back and then click elsewhere to move the cursor away from the word and bypass AutoCorrect.

Above: Word's AutoCorrect settings are hidden away in Word 2007–2010.

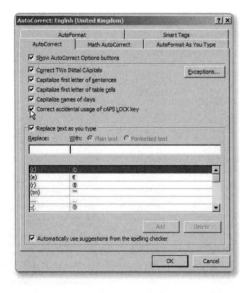

CUSTOMIZING AUTOCORRECT

There are a number of settings within Word's AutoCorrect that can be customized and switched on or off. All of these settings are displayed in an AutoCorrect dialogue box, which can be opened in pre-2007 versions of Word by clicking on the Tools menu and choosing AutoCorrect or AutoCorrect Options. In Word 2007, click on the multi-coloured Office button at the top-left corner of the screen, or in Word 2010, click on the File menu ribbon tab. In both cases a menu appears; click on Options or Word Options. From the dialogue box that appears, select Proofing from the list on the left and click on the AutoCorrect Options button in the main part of the dialogue box.

Capital Corrections and Exceptions

The AutoCorrect dialogue box has a tick box list of capital letter-related corrections that can be switched on or off. These help with the aforementioned problems of inadvertently typing with the Caps lock switched on and typing two capital letters at the start of a word.

Left: Word's AutoCorrect stores the settings for correcting the misuse of capital letters. These can be switched on or off.

AutoCorrect Exceptions

If there are some words and abbreviations that require two capital letters at the beginning (for example, IDs) or words that should be displayed in lower case (for example, mph), then these can be added to an Exceptions list. From within the AutoCorrect dialogue box, click on the Exceptions button and another dialogue box will appear. Click on the different tabs across the top of this dialogue box to add any relevant entries.

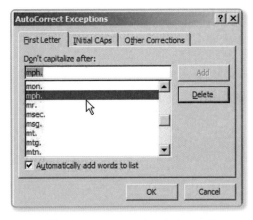

Above: Abbreviations can sometimes be incorrectly AutoCorrected, so a list of exceptions can be added.

Spelling Corrections

The reason why words such as 'Reveiw' are automatically changed to 'Review' can be found within a list in the AutoCorrect dialogue box. This list is in the lower half of the dialogue box and is alphabetically sorted. At the top of the list, there are some AutoCorrect entries for inserting

Hot Tip

The copyright, registered and trademark symbols (©,® and ™) can each be automatically created using AutoCorrect by typing in their respective letters in brackets. So, © is created by typing (c).

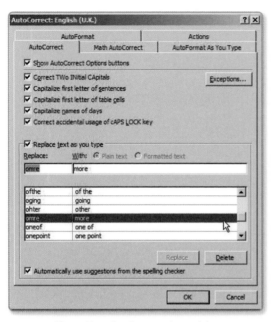

Above: Typical spelling mistakes and their corrections can be added in the AutoCorrect dialogue box. Entries can also be removed.

copyright and trademark symbols, but further down the list there are typical spelling mistakes and their corrections.

Removing AutoCorrect Spelling Corrections

If you want to remove an AutoCorrect spelling correction, select it from the list in the AutoCorrect dialogue box, then click on the Delete button. If you accidentally delete the wrong one, click on the Add button immediately and it will be re-entered. If, however, you want to add the correction at a later date, see the next section.

Adding Your Own AutoCorrect Spelling Corrections

Words that you frequently misspell can be added as an AutoCorrect entry to help save time when typing and reduce the risk of errors. From within the AutoCorrect dialogue box, enter the misspelled version of a word in the box to the left, underneath Replace. Enter the correct spelling in the box to the right. Click on the Add button and your entry will be listed.

AUTOMATIC FORMATTING

Open the AutoCorrect dialogue box and select the AutoFormat tab to see a variety of options for automatically formatting text as it is typed. For example, a website address can be converted into a hyperlink, so it can be clicked on to open the relevant web page (sometimes the Ctrl key has to be held down to activate the website address). There is also a tick box to ensure that fractions are automatically converted (so 1/2 becomes ½).

STORED WORDS AND SENTENCES

Word can store a wide range of words and sentences, which can be pasted into a document without having to type all of the words again. This is known as AutoText and can be customized to include your own words, phrases and paragraphs of text to help save time on repetitive typing of opening and closing sentences, the end of a letter and legal disclaimers.

Where Is AutoText in Word 2007–2010?

If you've used AutoText in Word 2003 or an earlier version and then upgraded to Word 2007 or 2010, AutoText may seem to have disappeared. It hasn't, but it has changed and is referred to as Building Blocks. In Word 2010, it can be found by clicking on the Insert ribbon tab, selecting the Quick Parts button and choosing AutoText for a list of existing AutoText. In Word 2007, an AutoText toolbar button needs to be added to the Quick Access Toolbar.

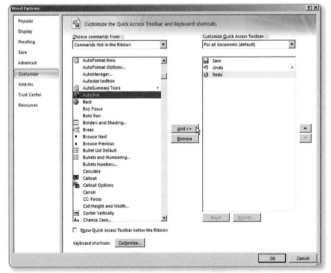

Adding an AutoText Button to the Quick Access Toolbar

Right click on the Quick Access Toolbar in the top-left corner of the screen and choose Customize Quick Access Toolbar. From the dialogue box that appears, click on the drop-down list near the top left and choose Commands Not in the Ribbon. Scroll down the list on the

Above: An AutoText toolbar button can be added to the Quick Access Toolbar in Word 2007–2010.

left and select AutoText (the list is alphabetically sorted). Click on the Add button in the middle of the box and AutoText will appear in the list on the right. Click on OK and check there is an AutoText button on the Quick Access Toolbar.

Where is AutoText in Word Pre-2007?

Click on the Insert menu, choose AutoText and a sub-menu will appear with a list of typical AutoText entries under further sub-menus. This can take some time to select and it's probably quicker to type the words than choose them from the menu, but once you know the AutoText words that are available, these pre-set words can be entered via the keyboard. See the next section for further details.

Press F3 for AutoText

In Word pre-2007, AutoText can be entered quickly via the keyboard. Type the first few letters of an AutoText entry, then press F3 on the keyboard. Word will check the AutoText entries and complete the word(s) if it recognizes which one you want. Otherwise, nothing will happen and you will need to type a few more letters. In some versions of Word, the AutoText entry is displayed above the cursor and the word(s) can be inserted by pressing Enter on the keyboard (also called the Return key).

Above: AutoText can be created in Word 2007–2010 by typing it into a document, selecting it and then adding it to the AutoText library.

Hot Tip

Create an AutoText entry by selecting the text to be used, then pressing Alt+F3 on the keyboard. A dialogue box will appear to create the entry.

Create Your Own AutoText Entries in Word 2007–2010

Type the text you want to repeatedly reuse in a document, making sure the layout (line spacing and paragraphs) is correct, then select the text. If the AutoText button has been added to the Quick Access Toolbar (see Adding an AutoText Button to the Quick Access Toolbar), click on this button and select Save Selection to AutoText Gallery. A small dialogue box will appear where the name of the AutoText entry can be changed and a description added. The name is the opening text that identifies the AutoText entry (the words that need to be typed before pressing F3 on the keyboard).

Create Your Own AutoText Entries in Word Pre-2007

Type the text you want to repeatedly reuse in a document, making sure the layout (line spacing and paragraphs) is correct, then select the text. Click on the Insert menu, choose AutoText and select New from the sub-menu. A small Create AutoText dialogue box will appear. The first few words of the selected text will be displayed, but these can be changed (these words have to be typed to activate the AutoText entry). Click on OK to create the entry, then make sure the AutoText has been created by typing those words and pressing F3 on the keyboard.

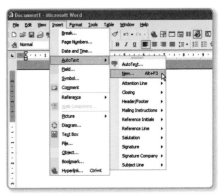

Above: AutoText can be created in Word pre-2007 by selecting the text to use, clicking on the Insert menu, selecting AutoText and choosing New from the sub-menu.

Delete an AutoText Entry

An AutoText entry can be used in every document when using Microsoft Word. If you want to remove an AutoText entry, there are a number of methods, depending on the version of Word in use:

- **Word 2007–2010:** Click on the AutoText toolbar button on the Quick Access Toolbar (see Adding an AutoText Button to the Quick Access Toolbar on page 127), position the mouse pointer over the AutoText entry, then right click and choose Organize and Delete. A dialogue box will appear. Select the AutoText entry and click on the Delete button.

- **Word pre-2007:** Click on the Insert menu, choose AutoText and select AutoText from the sub-menu. A dialogue box will appear with an alphabetically sorted list of AutoText entries. Select the entry to be removed, then click on the Delete button.

Hot Tip

In Word pre–2007, the program identifies AutoText as you type and displays a message if it recognizes an entry. When this happens, press Enter to insert the Autotext.

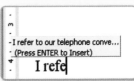

IDENTIFYING AND CORRECTING MISTAKES

Word has a number of tools to ensure the text in a document is correctly spelled and grammatically accurate. These can be useful if you know how to use them and how they can help to correct mistakes. The following section explains how Word checks your text as it is typed and how the program can help identify mistakes.

SPELLING MISTAKES

Word checks the spelling of the text as it is typed. After typing a word and pressing the space-bar, or Return key, Word will check the typed text and add a red wavy line underneath it if it determines it is incorrectly spelled. The program uses a dictionary to check spellings; if a word isn't in the dictionary, it is regarded as being misspelled.

Correcting a Spelling Mistake

When a red wavy line is displayed underneath a misspelled word, right click on the word and a shortcut menu will appear with a list of suggested words from which to choose. Word cannot always determine the correct spelling for a word, so it usually displays a list of suggestions, but in some cases it won't have any suggestions. A misspelled word can be quickly corrected by selecting one of the suggested words from the list.

I Always Misspell a Particular Word

If you find you frequently misspell a particular word and always have to right click on it and choose the correct spelling, try selecting the AutoCorrect option on the shortcut menu that appears. A sub-menu will appear with some correctly spelled words. Choose the correct spelling and Word will now remember to automatically correct the wrong spelling that has been typed with the correction that was selected. This is known as AutoCorrect and is covered in more detail towards the beginning of this chapter.

The Wrong Language

Text that has been copied from the Internet or from a document created by someone else may have the wrong language in use for the dictionary (for example, American English). Consequently, words such as organise may appear misspelled because the American version is organize. The language setting can be changed as follows:

Above: If the wrong language is used in Word, misspelled words won't be identified and correctly spelled words may be displayed as being wrong.

- ➔ **Word 2007–2010:** Right click on a misspelled word and choose Language to check which language is being used. If it is wrong, select Set Proofing Language and a dialogue box will appear with a list of languages. Choose the correct language and click on OK.

- ➔ **Word pre-2007:** Click on the Tools menu, select Language and choose Set Language from the sub-menu. A dialogue box will appear with a highlighted language at the top. If this is wrong, choose the correct one from the list, then click on OK.

DOUBLE WORDS

If a word is accidentally typed twice (for example, I am am here), a red wavy line will be displayed underneath the second word. Right click on this word and choose Delete Repeated Word to remove it.

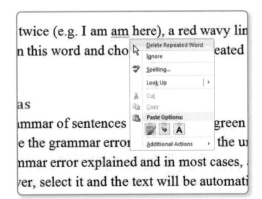

Above: If a word is accidentally typed twice in succession, Microsoft Word will display a red wavy line underneath it. Right click on the underlined word to remove it.

GRAMMAR DILEMMAS

Microsoft Word checks the grammar of sentences and displays a green wavy line underneath if it identifies a problem. To resolve the grammar error, right click on the underlined words and a shortcut menu will appear with the grammar error explained and, in most cases, a suggested answer. If you want to use the suggested answer, select it and the text will be automatically amended.

Above: Word's grammar checker can sometimes trip itself up. In this example, it has identified 'won't' as being incorrect but suggests replacing it with the same word!

Grammar Confusion

Sometimes, Word will find a grammatical error and provide a solution, which, when selected, will produce another grammatical error. In other cases, Word doesn't understand colloquial expressions or instances where a word starts with a capital letter within a sentence. If Word wrongly identifies a grammatical error, the suggested correction can be ignored by right clicking on it and choosing Ignore or Ignore Once.

Hot Tip

The green and red wavy lines that appear underneath words for spelling and grammatical errors do not appear when the document is printed, so they can remain on screen.

CHANGE A WORD

If a particular word has been used throughout a document and it needs to be changed to something else (for example, a person's name is Catherine, but it needs to be displayed as Kate), then Word's Find and Replace can do this in a few seconds. In Word pre-2007, click on the Edit menu and choose Find. In later versions of Word, click on the Home ribbon tab and select Replace from the top-right corner of the screen. From the dialogue box that appears, make sure the Replace tab is selected, then enter the word to find and the word with which to replace it. Click on the Replace All button to change all these words in the document.

Press Ctrl+H to open the Find and Replace dialogue box.

Above: If a word needs to be changed several times throughout a document, use Find and Replace to do this in a matter of seconds.

I NEED ANOTHER WORD

Sometimes you can't think of another word to use with the same meaning, but Microsoft Word can often save the day with its built-in thesaurus. In most versions of Word, right click on the word and choose Synonyms. A sub-menu will appear with some suggested alternatives to select, or click on Thesaurus and a dialogue box or panel will appear with further options. In early versions of Word, highlight the word you want to change, click on the Tools menu, choose Language and select Thesaurus from the sub-menu. A small dialogue box will appear with some suggested alternatives from which to choose.

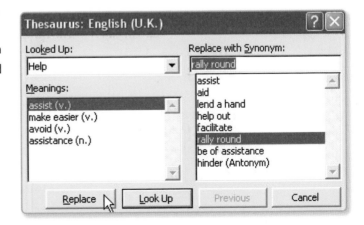

Right: Word's thesaurus can help find different words and use them in a document. This dialogue box is used in Word pre-2007.

KNOW YOUR DOCUMENT DATA

If a document has to be written with a maximum or minimum number of words or pages, Microsoft Word can quickly help to keep track of this information and display it on the page or on the screen. The following section explains how to use these tools in a Word document.

COUNTING WORDS

Word counts are useful for making sure you've written enough or not too much in a document or a section of a document. Microsoft Word can display the number of words in a document or selected block of text as follows:

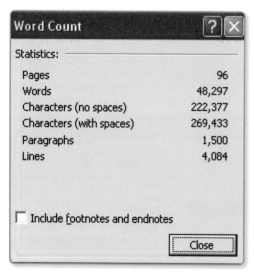

Above: The Word Count box appears in Word pre-2007 displaying the number of words in a document or in selected text.

→ **Word 2007–2010:** The number of words in the document is always displayed in the bottom-left corner of the screen. When some text is selected, the word count for the selection is displayed, followed by the word count for the entire document (for example, 5/1250 means there are five words in the selected text and 1,250 words in the whole document).

→ **Word pre-2007:** Click on the Tools menu and choose Word Count. A dialogue box will appear displaying the number of words in the document or, if some text has been selected, the number of words in the selected text.

Displaying a Word Count on a Page

The number of words in a document can be displayed anywhere in a document (for example, at the top or bottom). To include a word count in a document, position the cursor at the point where it is going to be displayed, then, in Word pre-2007, click on the Insert menu and choose Field. In later versions of Word, click on the Insert ribbon tab, select Quick Parts and choose Field from the sub-menu. In all cases a dialogue box will appear. Under the Document Information category, select the field called NumWords. Choose a format for how the word count will be displayed (click on the Options button in Word pre-2007), then click on OK.

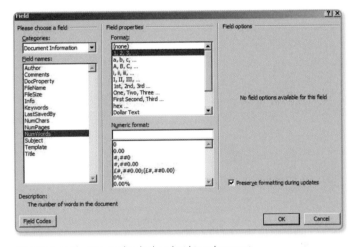

Above: A word count can be displayed within a document by creating a field (picture shows Word 2010).

Updating a Word Count in a Document

When a word count is displayed within a document, it doesn't automatically update whenever a new word is typed in the document or a word is deleted. The word count will update whenever the document is opened and it can be manually updated by right clicking on the number displayed and choosing Update Field.

HOW MANY PAGES?

The number of pages within a document is displayed in the bottom-left corner of the screen along with the page number that is currently on the screen. For example, 2/8 displayed in the bottom-left corner of the screen means page two is currently on the screen and there are a total of eight pages.

CHECKING FOR CHANGES

When a Word document is edited by you or someone else, it's often useful to know what has been changed or what was originally written. Word can quickly display these changes to show the differences by using Track Changes. The following section shows how to use Word's Track Changes tools.

TRACK CHANGES

Track Changes is a useful feature in Word that can show all the editing that has been made to a document. It's particularly useful if a document is changed by someone else and returned to the original author to review those changes. Any text that has been deleted, added or changed is displayed in different colours.

Switching on Track Changes in Word 2007-2010
Click on the Review ribbon tab and select the Track Changes button. The button will now be highlighted, indicating Track Changes is switched on. Try changing some text in the document, deleting a word or adding new text. All of these changes will be displayed in a different colour. Deleted text will either remain on screen with a line through it (strikethrough) or disappear from the screen, but a message box will be displayed to the right. Click on the Track Changes button on the Review ribbon tab again to switch off Track Changes.

Switching on Track Changes in Word Pre-2007
Click on the Tools menu and select Track Changes. If a sub-menu appears, select Highlight Changes and a dialogue box will

Hot Tip
Switch Track Changes on and off by holding down the Ctrl and Shift keys on the keyboard and pressing E.

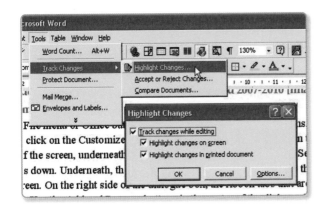

appear. Add a tick mark to the option labelled Track changes while editing, then click on OK. Try changing some text in the document, deleting a word or adding new text. All of these changes will be displayed in a different colour. Deleted text will either remain on screen with a line through it (strikethrough) or disappear from the screen, but a message box will be displayed to the right. Return to the Tools menu and choose Track Changes again to switch it off.

Checking a Document with Track Changes

Word pre-2007 has a Reviewing toolbar that provides a number of useful buttons that can be used to view all the changes made to a document, move between each change and accept or reject each or all of the changes. Word 2007–2010 has a Reviewing pane (click on the Review ribbon tab and select the Reviewing pane button), which is displayed down the left side of the screen and lists all of the changes made to a document. These changes are grouped into changes in the main part of the document, the header and footer, text boxes, footnotes and endnotes.

Hot Tip

Look at the bottom of the screen in Word pre-2007 for the letters TRK on the status bar. Double click here to switch Track Changes on and off.

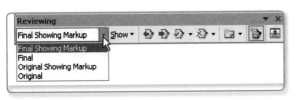

Changing the Colours and Track Changes Features

The colours used when deleting text, adding text and editing text when track changes is switched on can be altered. Look for an Options button in the Track Changes dialogue box or something similar on the Track Changes menu or sub-menu. A dialogue box will provide a number of colour options for different types of amendments (inserted text, deleted text).

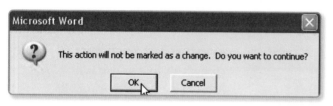

Above: When a change is made to a document that cannot be tracked, a message box will appear.

Changes That Cannot Be Tracked

Some changes cannot be tracked in Word. For example, if a row or column in a table is deleted, Word cannot record this action under Track Changes. When this happens, a message box will appear warning that the changes made cannot be tracked. Click on OK to continue or Cancel to reverse the change.

Accepting and Rejecting Changes

Individual changes can be accepted or rejected by right clicking on each one and choosing the appropriate option from the shortcut menu that appears. Depending on the version of Word, use the Reviewing toolbar buttons or buttons on the Review ribbon tab to move between changes and accept or reject them. There are also various views available, including the Final and Original versions with or without Markup (changes). These settings help to show what has been changed.

Sending a Document for Editing with Track Changes

If you want to send a document to someone to check through it and make amendments, but you want to be able to see those amendments when the document is returned, switch on track changes and warn the recipient that any changes made will appear in a different colour. When the document is returned, you will be able to see the changes made. If the recipient accidentally switches off track changes, see the next section for a solution.

Comparing an Original and Amended Document in Word 2007-2010

If track changes does not work or a document is amended, but you still have the original, then Word can compare two documents and highlight the differences. Click on the Review ribbon tab, select the Compare button (top right of the screen) and choose Compare. A small dialogue box will appear, allowing you to locate and choose the two documents to compare and customize how the differences are displayed.

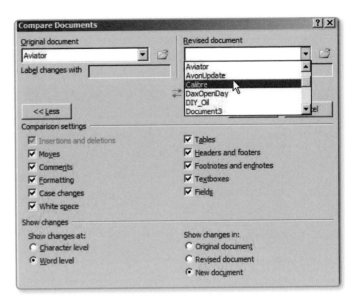

Above: Word can compare two documents and highlight the differences, which is useful if a document has been edited and you want to compare it against the original.

Hot Tip

If several people edit a document, all of the changes can be reviewed in Word 2007–2010. Click on Compare on the Review ribbon tab and select Combine.

Comparing an Original and Amended Document in Word Pre-2007

If track changes does not work or a document is amended, but you still have the original, then Word can compare two documents and highlight the differences. Make sure one of the document is open (the original or the amended version), then click on the Tools menu and choose Compare and Merge Documents or select Track Changes and choose Compare Documents from the sub-menu. A dialogue box will appear where you can locate the document to compare and click on Open, or Merge. All of the differences will be highlighted in a similar way to track changes. These differences can be accepted and rejected using the same track changes methods.

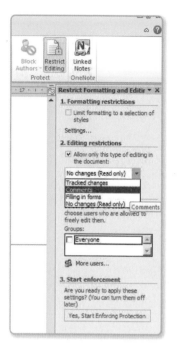

Left: The editing of a document in Word 2010 can be restricted to specific formatting and specific people.

CONTROLLING CHANGES

Word 2010 can restrict the type of editing that can be performed on a particular document. Click on the Review ribbon tab and select Restrict Editing to see a list of options displayed down the right side of the screen. Formatting and editing restrictions can be applied and specific users can have more rights over others.

COMMENTING ON A DOCUMENT

Another approach to editing a document is to add comments at specific points in the text. Each comment is stored separately from the main text but can be easily spotted. The content of each comment is displayed to the side or below the document.

Inserting a Comment

Position the cursor where the comment needs to be added, click on the Insert menu and choose Comment or click on the Review ribbon tab in Word 2007–2010 and select the New Comment button. In all cases a Comments window will appear at the bottom of the screen or a box will appear to the right. Text can be typed into this comment area and a comment marker will appear in the text. After typing some information for the comment, click elsewhere in the main part of the text to continue editing.

Above: Comments can be viewed by clicking on this option on the Show or Show Markup button on the Review tab or Reviewing toolbar.

Reading Comments

If a comment within a document appears only as a marker over a word or series of words, try hovering the mouse pointer over it and the entire comment may be displayed on screen. Otherwise, try right clicking on the comment and choosing Edit Comment. The Reviewing toolbar in Word pre-2007, or Review ribbon tab in Word 2007–2010, has a number of buttons to be able to read each comment and show all of them on screen.

Deleting Comments

A comment can be quickly deleted by right clicking on it and choosing Delete Comment. There is also a Delete Comment toolbar button on the Reviewing toolbar or Review ribbon tab.

UNDERSTANDING A DOCUMENT

Large documents can become difficult to understand, especially their structure and where all the headings should be used. This is even more difficult when a document has been written by someone else. Luckily, Word has some useful tools to help understand the contents and structure of a document.

OUTLINE THE HEADINGS

If a document contains several headings and different heading levels (for example, Heading 1, Heading 2 and so on), then Word's Outline view can help to see all of these headings to understand the structure of the document. Click on the View menu or ribbon tab and choose Outline. A new set of toolbar or ribbon buttons will appear along the top of the screen and the view of the document will change.

Change the Heading View in Outline

With Outline view on the screen, click on the numbered buttons to display certain heading levels, or click on the drop-down list for Show Level and select a heading level to be displayed. For example,

Left: The outline view of a document helps to see all the headings with or without the text.

if Heading 3 is selected, then Headings 3, 2 and 1 will all be displayed (without any other headings or text). This method can help to see the main headings in a document and understand its structure, but only works if a document has been created with heading levels.

Expanding and Collapsing Headings

Click on the plus or minus symbols next to any headings listed in Outline view to see more or fewer headings and text. This can help to see top level headings or all the headings in a document.

MAPS AND NAVIGATION

Although viewing a document in Outline view will help to see the structure of headings used, it becomes a little clumsy when you try to edit the text and move around the document. A Document Map or Navigation pane is often an easier solution. It allows a list of headings to be displayed down the left-hand side of the screen, leaving the main text in the document to remain on screen in a familiar page layout, normal or draft view. In Word pre-2007, click on the View menu and choose Document Map. In later versions of Word, click on the View ribbon tab and add a tick mark next to Navigation pane.

Right: A Document Map or Navigation pane can be used to see a list of headings used throughout a document.

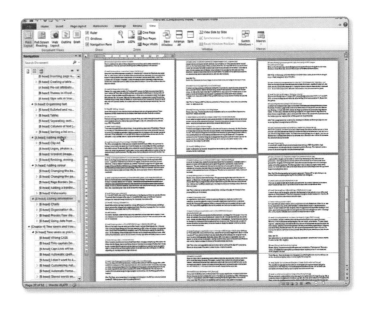

> **Hot Tip**
>
> If some text doesn't have a heading level, select it and hold down the Ctrl and Alt keys, then press 1 to convert it to Heading 1, 2 to convert it to Heading 2 or 3 for Heading 3.

Using the Document Map or Navigation Pane

A Document Map or Navigation pane is similar to the contents page of a book. It lists the headings in a document, providing heading levels have been used (for example, Heading 1, Heading 2). Click on any of the headings listed in the Document Map or Navigation pane and Word will immediately jump to that point in the document.

Hot Tip

Outline view and a Document Map or Navigation pane only work if heading levels are used in a document. See Headings in chapter three for further details.

Expanding and Collapsing Levels

Click on the triangles or plus/minus symbols next to any headings listed in the Document Map or Navigation pane. Any headings within this heading will be expanded or collapsed. This can help to see top-level headings or all the headings in a document.

Resizing a Document Map or Navigation Pane

Hover the mouse pointer over the dividing line between the document and the Document Map or Navigation pane. When it changes to a double-headed arrow, hold the left button down and move the mouse pointer to the left or right to change the width of the Document Map or Navigation pane. Release the left button to stop resizing it.

Removing a Document Map or Navigation Pane

Click on the Insert menu and choose Document Map or click on the View ribbon tab and remove the tick mark from the box next to Navigation pane.

AUTOMATIC SUMMARY

Word 2007 and previous versions include a tool that can analyse a document and extract the headings, keywords and main points, creating a summary or highlighting them within the document. It's called AutoSummarize, but was discontinued in Word 2010. In Word 2003 and earlier versions, AutoSummarize is found on the Tools menu. After selecting it from the menu, a dialogue box will appear with a number of options for how the summary of the document should be created. For example, a summary could highlight the key points in the document, hide the main text and display only a summary or produce a summary in a separate document.

Where is AutoSummarize in Word 2007?

Click on the Office button in the top-left corner of the screen and from the menu that drops down, choose Word Options.

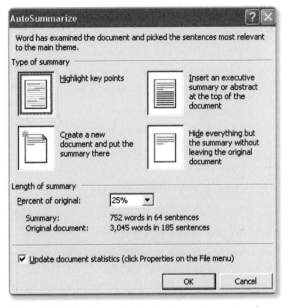

Above: Word's AutoSummarize tool analyses a document and either highlights the main points or displays a summary.

A dialogue box will appear. Click on Customize on the left side and click on the drop-down list under the section Choose commands from. Select Commands not in the Ribbon, then look below in the list of commands for Auto Summary Tools. Once found, select Auto Summary Tools and click on the Add button. This will now appear in the list on the right. Click on OK to return to the document and an Auto Summary button will be displayed on the Quick Access Toolbar. Click on this to summarize a document.

BOOKMARKS

Specific points in a document can be marked with a bookmark, making them easier to find or return to in the future. A bookmark is denoted by a name, so use one that is relevant and easy to remember. To create a bookmark, select a word or number of words (if the word or words are deleted, the bookmark will be removed), then click on the Insert menu or ribbon tab (Word 2007–2010) and select Bookmark. From the dialogue box that appears, enter a name for the bookmark and click on OK.

Hot Tip

Bookmark names can consist of more than one word, but cannot have spaces between them. For example, a bookmark name for the first chapter has to be written as Chapter1 or Chapter_1, not Chapter 1.

Jumping to Bookmarks

Bookmarks need to be quick and easy to access, otherwise it would be just as quick to scroll through a document. The fastest method of using a bookmark is to press F5 on the keyboard and a dialogue box will appear. Make sure the Go To tab is selected and choose Bookmark from the list on the left. Select the bookmark you want to go to from the list on the right, then click on the Go To button. The dialogue box will close and the document will move to the bookmark.

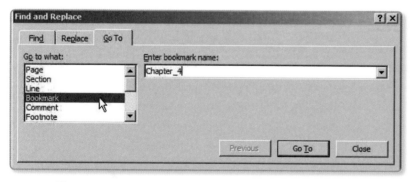

Above: Bookmarks can be quickly accessed by pressing F5 on the keyboard.

Deleting Bookmarks

Click on the Insert menu or ribbon tab (Word 2007–2010) and select Bookmark. From the dialogue box that appears, select the bookmark you want to remove and click on the Delete button. The bookmark will be deleted, but the text to which it is linked will not be removed from the document. Click on the Close button to return to the document.

WORD BETWEEN WORK AND HOME

Word documents can be shared between work and home, even if you have different versions of the program. The following section outlines some of the best methods and potential problems with sharing your documents between work and home.

VERSION CONFLICTS

One of the biggest problems with using Microsoft Word at home and at work is that in most cases, the version of Word at home won't be the same as the one at work. We have outlined some of the main differences in chapter one. However, you may find some features are not available. For example, AutoSummarize isn't available in Word 2010, but is available in earlier versions.

My Word Files Won't Open at Home

In most situations, if a Word file or document cannot be opened, it has been created in Word 2007 or 2010 and will have a .docx extension at the end of its name (for example, Report.docx). There are two solutions to this problem, which are outlined as follows:

➔ At work, resave the document as a Word 97–2003 document (open the document and press F12 to resave), which can be opened in earlier versions of Word.

Above: Resaving a Word document as an earlier version or as RTF (Rich Text Format) often allows the file to be opened in other programs or earlier versions of Word.

⊙ At home, visit http://support.microsoft.com/kb/924074 via the Internet and download a Microsoft Office Compatibility Pack to allow Word 2007–2010 files with a .docx extension to be opened in earlier versions of the program.

I Don't Have Word at Home

Many other word processors can open Word documents and we have listed some of the free programs in chapter one. You may have to return to work and resave the Word document, especially if you are using Word 2007–2010. With the document open in Word, press F12 on the keyboard to open the Save As dialogue box. Under Save as Type (near the bottom of the dialogue box) change the file type to Word 97–2003 or Rich Text Format (this is compatible with the majority of word processors and other programs), then click on the Save button.

Opening a Word Document in Other Programs

A Word document can be used in many other programs, ranging from desktop publishing software for creating a newsletter or magazine, to web design software for creating a website. However, the document may need to be saved in a more compatible format. File types such as Rich Text Format (RTF) and Text (TXT) are more compatible with a wider range of programs.

SENDING A DOCUMENT HOME

There are a number of methods of enabling a Word document at work to be used at home. Here are some of the popular methods:

⊙ **Remote access:** If you can access your work's computers and servers from home via the Internet, then this is one of the quickest methods of using a Word document at home.

⊙ **Email:** At work, click on the File menu or Ribbon tab (Office button in Word 2007) in Word and select Send To, followed by Mail Recipient, or select Save & Send and then select Send as Attachment. Your email program will open with the Word document

Above: A document can be emailed from within Microsoft Word by clicking on the File menu, ribbon tab or Office button.

Up-To-Date Documents

Keeping track of the most up-to-date version of a document can become complicated when sharing a file between home and work. Saving the document as a different name with a version number can help, but Word can also help with retrieving information on when a document was last accessed and modified. With the document open in Word, click on the File menu or Ribbon tab (Office button in Word 2007). In Word 2007–2010, select Info; in earlier versions, select Properties. In all cases, information on when the document was last accessed and modified will be displayed.

attached. Providing you have an email address that can be accessed from home, the file can be sent and opened at home.

Memory stick: Save the Word document on to a memory stick or similar storage device. Some work places do not allow this practice because of the threat of viruses.

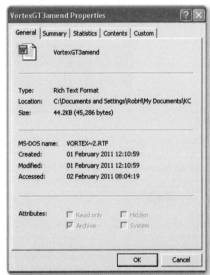

Above: Document properties can sometimes help to determine the most up-to-date version of a file.

TYPICAL PROBLEMS

Problems can occur in Word, just like any computer program. Whilst some are caused by user error, some are traits of the software. The following pages cover some of the typical troubles most people experience and how they can usually be resolved.

FORMATTING DILEMMAS

The early versions of Word gained a reputation for seemingly changing the font and size of text without warning. However, there are several explanations for this and some solutions to resolve many of the typical problems that can arise concerning the formatting of text in a document.

I Can't See the Text I'm Typing

The font colour is probably the same as the page colour. Press Ctrl+D on the keyboard and a Font dialogue box will appear. Look at the setting for Font color and make sure it's not the same as the page colour.

The Text Keeps Changing to Bold or Another Font and Size

This usually happens at the bottom of the text. One of the quickest ways to fix this when typing is to hold down the Ctrl key and press the space

> **Hot Tip**
> Bold can be switched on and off by holding down the Ctrl key on the keyboard and pressing B.

bar. The default font settings will be restored and hopefully this means the bold will be switched off and the font settings set to standard.

I Can't Understand Any of the Words I'm Typing

A font type such as Windings is probably being used. Press Ctrl+D on the keyboard and the Font dialogue box will appear. Look at the Font displayed and change it to something else, such as Times New Roman.

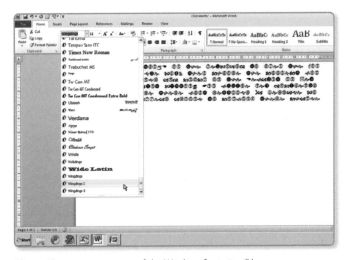

When I Press Return, the Line Spacing Is Too Big

The spacing before and after each paragraph needs to be adjusted. Select the text that has been

Above: If some text uses one of the Windings fonts, it will become illegible and the font will have to be changed for it to be read.

affected, right click inside it and choose Paragraph. From the dialogue box that appears, change the settings for Spacing Before and After.

The Font Settings Are Wrong When I Create a New Document

Press Ctrl+D on the keyboard to open the Font dialogue box, then choose the correct font settings and click on the Default or Set as Default button. All future new documents will use these font settings (a message box may appear asking to confirm these changes).

SCREEN DISASTERS

The layout of the screen and its contents can sometimes be displayed incorrectly. Here are some of the typical problems that can arise and how to fix them.

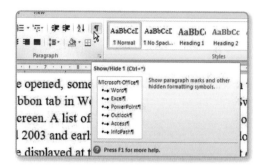

Above: Show/Hide reveals the traditional formatting markers to identify spaces and returns at the end of paragraphs. These can be switched off by clicking on the toolbar button shown here.

There Are Dots between Words and Markers at the End of Some Lines

The on-screen markers that indicate spaces and ends of paragraphs are being shown on the document, but won't be visible if the document is printed. This is known as Show/Hide and there is a toolbar button that switches it on and off. Alternatively, hold down the Ctrl and Shift keys and press the number 8 to switch it on and off.

My Toolbar Buttons Are Missing

In Word pre-2007, right click on any toolbar button or menu and a checklist of toolbars will appear. Add tick marks to any of the toolbars required and they will appear on screen. In Word 2007–2010, look for a small arrow pointing downwards in the top-right corner of the screen. Click on this arrow and the ribbon buttons will reappear. Alternatively, right click on any of the ribbon tabs (Home, Insert, View) and a shortcut menu will appear with a tick mark against Minimize the ribbon. Select this option to remove the tick mark and reveal the ribbon buttons.

The Toolbars Are All on One Line with Some Buttons Missing

This is only applicable to Word pre-2007. Look along the toolbar buttons for a small button that looks like two arrows pointing to the right (>>) and one triangle pointing down. Click on this button and a palette of buttons will appear, plus a few menu options. Select Show Buttons on Two Rows.

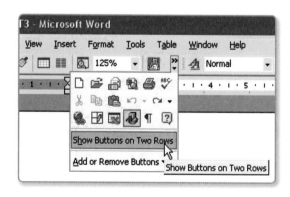

Above: Toolbar buttons in Word pre-2007 can be separated on to two rows.

A Toolbar Is in the Wrong Position

This is only applicable to Word pre-2007. If a toolbar is in the middle of the screen, hover the tip of the mouse pointer over its title bar (along the top), hold the left button down and move the toolbar to the correct location. If a toolbar is incorrectly positioned around an edge of the screen, look for an embossed line or two lines on the side of the toolbar. Position the tip of the mouse pointer over this line or lines, hold the left button down and move the mouse to move the toolbar.

The Task Pane Has Disappeared in Word 2002-2003

Word 2002 and 2003 use a Task pane displayed on the right-hand side of the screen, which includes various panes for opening files, copying data and inserting ClipArt (Word 2003 has more options than 2002). This Task pane can be displayed or hidden by clicking on the View menu and selecting Task Pane.

I've Upgraded to Word 2007-2010 and Can't Find Anything!

Word 2007 and 2010 can initially be a love or hate relationship when used for the first time, especially if you've upgraded from Word 2003 or an earlier version. The menus have been replaced with ribbon tabs along the top of the screen, which display different sets of ribbon buttons. Most of the familiar Word features can be found via these ribbon tabs and buttons. There is also a Quick Access Toolbar in the top-left corner of the screen, which can be customized to add or remove buttons. This book covers all versions of Word, so it can help to upgrade to a later version of Word.

The File, View and Other Menus are below the Toolbars

This is only applicable to Word pre-2007. Position the mouse pointer to the left of the File menu. When it changes to a cross with four arrows, hold the left button down and move up the screen to move the menu bar up and above the toolbar buttons. When it has moved to the correct position, release the left button on the mouse.

The Menus in Word 2000-2003 Have Several Options Missing

In Word 2000, 2002 and 2003, the menus (File, Edit, View, and so on) are often shorter than they should be because they only list the recently used options. If a particular option is missing, move the mouse pointer down to the bottom of the menu and hover it over two arrows pointing downwards. The menu will be extended to reveal all of its options.

Hot Tip

Hold down the Alt key on the keyboard and press the Tab key to switch between programs and files.

There Are + and - Symbols next to the Headings

The Outline view has been selected, which allows the text to be compressed to the headings. Click on the View menu or ribbon tab and select Print Layout or Page Layout to close this view.

FILE TROUBLE

Word documents can disappear off screen, refuse to open in later versions of the program and display worrying warnings about compatibility. Here are some of the common problems and solutions.

Where Are the Documents I've Just Opened?

When two or more Word documents are opened, some of them will not be visible on the screen, but they are still open. Click on the View ribbon tab in Word 2007–2010 and select the Switch Windows ribbon button near the top right of the screen. A list of the Word documents that are open will be displayed; select one to see it. In Word 2003 and earlier versions, click on the Window menu and a list of the open Word documents will be displayed at the bottom of the menu; select one of them to see it on the screen.

I Can't Remember the Name of the File I've Just Closed

Click on the File menu, ribbon tab or Office button (Word 2007) and select Recent in Word 2007–2010 or look at the bottom of the menu in earlier versions. A list of the recently opened documents will be displayed. They are displayed in date order with the latest at the top. Select one of them to open it.

Word Cannot Open a File

There are several reasons why Word cannot open a file at times. Here are some of the common ones:

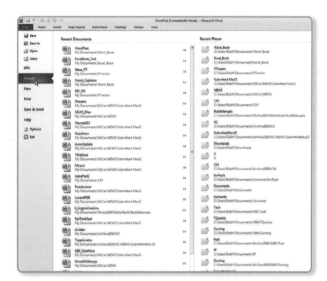

Above: Word displays a list of recently opened documents, which can help to find a file if you've forgotten its name or location.

➔ **Different file format**: If a file has been created in another program, then its file format (the type of file it is) may be incompatible. Return to the program in which the file was created and try to see if it can be saved as a Word document or something similar (RTF, TXT).

➔ **Later version**: Word documents created in Word 2007 and 2010 will have a .docx extension at the end of their filename. Earlier versions of Word cannot open these files unless they have a compatibility pack from http://support.microsoft.com/kb/924074 or the file is saved as a Word 97–2003 type.

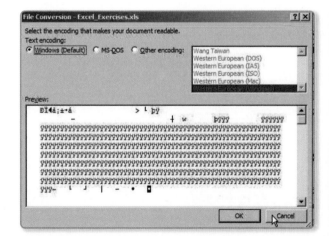

Above: Try opening an Excel file in Word 2010 and the program will do its best to help, but it really is the wrong program to use.

CREATING PROFESSIONAL DOCUMENTS

WRITE A DISSERTATION, THESIS OR BOOK

Word can help write a long and complicated document, with chapters, headings and sub-headings, references, footnotes, a contents page and index. The following step-by-step guide shows how to create the structure of such a document.

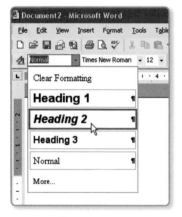

Above: Headings can be selected in Word pre-2007 via the Formatting toolbar.

1. Decide upon a structure of chapters, headings and sub-headings for the document. Word uses Headings, which are sorted in numerical order (Heading 1, Heading 2, Heading 3) and can be applied to a document to create a structure to it. Heading 1, for example, is a top-level heading, which may be used for the chapter headings. Heading 2 can be used for the main headings throughout the document and Heading 3 can be used for the sub-headings.

2. Applying Word's heading levels to different headings throughout a document can be completed as you write the document, or if you've already written them, they can be applied afterwards.

3. Select the text for the heading or the point at the document where the heading will be written, then choose the heading level (for example, Heading 1, Heading 2) from the Home ribbon tab in Word 2007–2010 or the Formatting toolbar in earlier versions of Word.

Hot Tip

Hold down the Ctrl+Alt keys and press 1 to apply Heading 1, press 2 for Heading 2 and 3 for Heading 3.

Above: A table of contents (TOC) is created in Word 2007–2010 by clicking on the appropriate button in the References ribbon tab.

4. As the document builds up with headings, a table of contents can be inserted at the front to keep track of the document's structure. Position the cursor at a point in the document where the table of contents (TOC) needs to be created. You may want to add an empty page (press Ctrl+Enter on the keyboard).

5. To add a table of contents in Word 2007–2010, click on the References ribbon tab and select the Table of Contents button (top-left corner of the screen). A list of TOC styles will appear. Choose one of them and a table of contents will appear in the document.

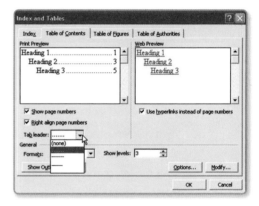

Above: In Word pre-2007, a table of contents (TOC) is created using a dialogue box with options for styles and settings.

6. To add a table of contents in Word pre-2007, click on the Insert menu, choose Index and Tables, or Reference followed by Index and Tables. An Index and Tables dialogue box will appear. Select the Table of Contents tab, then choose a style for the TOC and check the settings are correct. Click on OK to create the table of contents in the document.

7. If an index needs to be created at the end of the document, the first step is to mark some entries to be included in it. Start at the beginning of the document and select a word to be included in the index.

Hot Tip

Hold down the Ctrl key on the keyboard and left click on a heading listed in the TOC to jump to that point in the document.

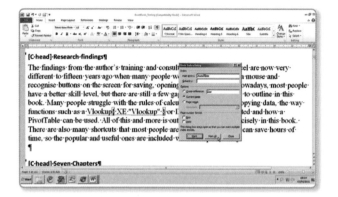

Above: Keywords within a document need to be marked before an index can be created.

8. Press Alt+Shift+X on the keyboard and a Mark Index Entry dialogue box will appear. The selected word will appear at the top of the dialogue box, next to Main entry. Make sure Current page is selected, then click on Mark All for Word to check through the document for every instance where this word appears and include them in the index, or Mark (Word will only include this instance in the index).

9. With the Mark Index Entry dialogue box still on the screen, move down the document and select another word to include in the index. Click inside the dialogue box and click on the Mark button or the Mark All button. Some code will appear next to each marked text, but this isn't visible when printed.

10. Once all relevant text has been marked for the index, close the Mark Index Entry dialogue box. Move to the end of the document (press Ctrl+End), then click on the References ribbon tab in Word 2007–2010 and select the Insert Index button or, in Word pre-2007, click on the Insert menu, choose Index and Tables, or Reference followed by Index and Tables from the sub-menu. In all cases, a dialogue box will appear.

Hot Tip

After marking entries for an index, space and paragraph markers will appear throughout the document. Press Ctrl+Shift+8 to hide them.

11. Make sure the Index tab is selected in the dialogue box, then choose some settings for the index (number of columns, right-aligned page numbers). Click on OK to close the dialogue box and insert the index into the document.

12. The index and table of contents can both be updated by right clicking inside them and choosing Update Field. If new words need to be added to the index, mark these entries (see steps 7–9), then update the index and they will be automatically added. Similarly, if new headings are inserted in the document, these will be automatically added to the table of contents upon updating it.

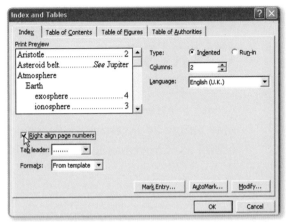

Above: Once all the keywords in a document have been marked, an index can be created.

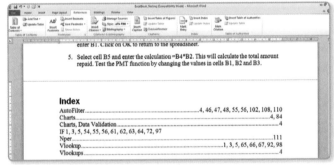

Above: An index created in Word looks professional and can be updated whenever the document changes or new text is added to it.

An index or table of contents can be deleted by swiping the mouse pointer over it with the left button held down. Once all of it has been selected, press Delete on the keyboard.

FURTHER INFORMATION IN THIS BOOK

Headings: Chapter 3, pages 90–92

Inserting a table of contents: Chapter 3, pages 93–94

Understanding a document: Chapter 4, pages 142–146

Creating an index: Chapter 6, pages 228–229

SEND A PERSONALIZED CHRISTMAS LETTER

Create a letter to send to numerous people and personalize it with Word's mail merge by inserting their name and address details. This is not only useful for Christmas letters, but also invitations and announcements.

Above: Microsoft Excel can be used to create a list of people and their contact details, which can in turn be used by Word's Mail Merge to produce a personalized newsletter.

Above: Mail Merge in Word pre-2007 can be found on the Tools menu or on a sub-menu of the Tools menu.

1. Before starting to write a Christmas letter, decide on how you are going to organize and use the list of recipients and their address details. The list can be created in Word, retrieved from Outlook's contacts or stored in a program such as Excel. Whatever the method, the list can be reused each year and people can be added and removed from it.

2. If you intend to create a list of people and their addresses in Word, this will be stored in a separate document, but can be created during the mail merge. The list can be amended at any time in the future to add more people or remove existing people, plus it can be used every year.

3. If you want to create a list of people in Excel, open the program and write some headings across the top of the worksheet,

such as first name, surname, address1, address2, postcode. Enter the details for each person to whom you want to send a Christmas, using one row for each person's details. Save the file as a standard Excel file.

4. When you're ready to produce the Christmas letter and run a mail merge, activate Mail Merge in Word. Depending on the version of Word you are using, either click on the Tools menu (Word pre-2007) and choose Mail Merge, or Letters and Mailings followed by Mail Merge Wizard (*see* picture opposite), or click on the Mailings ribbon tab (Word 2007–2010) and a number of ribbon buttons will appear across the top of the screen for mail merging.

5. In Word pre-2007, mail merge is a series of step-by-step procedures, starting with a choice of a main document (choose a letter), followed by selecting the list of recipients or creating a list in Word. If a list of recipients is created in Word, you can choose the categories of information (name, surname, address), which are called fields, then enter all the data for each recipient.

6. In Word 2007–2010, click on the Start Mail Merge button and choose Letters. Next, click on the Select Recipients button and choose

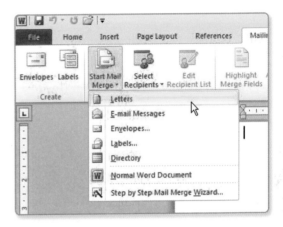

Above: Mail Merge in Word 2007–2010 is found on the Mailings ribbon tab. Select the Start Mail Merge button and choose Letters to create a personalized Christmas letter.

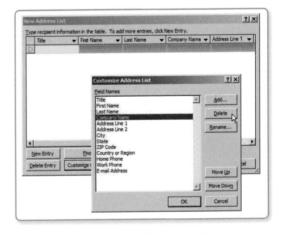

Above: The contact details for all the people who will receive the Christmas letter can be stored in Word and used again in the future. Word has a standard set of headings for storing this information (First Name, Last Name), which can be changed or removed.

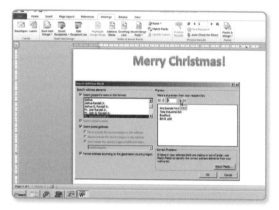

Above: An Address Block can be inserted into a Mail Merge, which saves time adding all the address details and making sure they are all correctly positioned.

Above: A letter can be personalized by entering merge fields such as the recipient's name or surname and their town or city.

a source for the recipients' information. If a list of the recipients needs to be created, select Type New List and follow the on-screen instructions for entering the information for each recipient and changing any of the information categories (name, surname, address).

7. Once the recipients have either been selected from an existing source or created, you're ready to start writing the Christmas letter. Create the letter in the same way as any other letter, but when you want to display the recipient's address, click on an option for the address block, which will help to correctly enter each person's address details. Similarly, a Greeting Line can ensure each letter starts with Dear, followed by the recipient's first name.

8. Other information for each recipient can be included in the letter by clicking on an option or button such as Insert Merge Field. This may be on a toolbar, ribbon or task pane, depending on the version of Word you are using.

9. Once the Christmas letter has been created and all the necessary categories of information included, you now have a main document (a master copy), of which multiple copies can be created, with individual recipient's information displayed in each copy. Click on a button or option to complete the mail merge and preview all the pages.

10. There will now be at least two documents open in Word. One of the documents will be the main document containing the Christmas letter and the different categories of information for the recipients. The other document will be much longer and contain a copy of the main document for each recipient. Each page in this document can be changed, so if you find any mistakes, they can be rectified.

Above: The merged contact details can be viewed before all of the Christmas letters are printed. In Word 2007–2010, click on the Preview Results button.

11. When you're ready to print your Christmas letters, make sure the longer document is on screen, then print them out. You may want to open the Print Preview screen first to check all the pages are correct before printing them. If you spot some mistakes, then close the Print Preview screen and return to the Normal or Print Layout view to make any corrections.

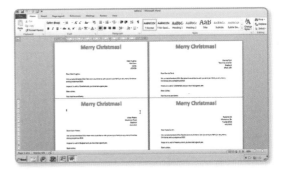

Above: Once the mail merge has been done, there will be multiple copies of the main document, each one personalized with a different recipient's details. These documents can be individually edited and printed.

12. If you created a recipient list in Word, the program will have already prompted you to save it and this file can be used again in the future for other letters. You may not want to save the Christmas letter's main document or all the copies created from the mail merge because they will be different for the next Christmas letter, but if you do choose to save them, they will be saved as normal Word documents.

FURTHER INFORMATION IN THIS BOOK

Mail merge: Chapter 6, pages 204–208

CREATE A WEB PAGE

A Word document can be converted into a web page with images and text, then viewed using a web browser such as Internet Explorer. The following step-by-step guide shows how to create such a file in Word and open it in a web browser.

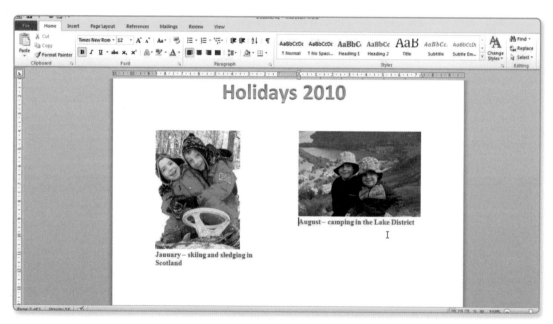

Above: A web page can be created from a Word document containing images and text.

1. If you already have a document open, which you want to convert to a web page, then skip this step. Otherwise, open a new document and add the content you want to display on the web page (text, tables, images).

2. Keep the web page simple and try to limit its length to one page. If there are lots of text and images, display them inside a table so that it can be organized and will be correctly positioned when the document is converted to a web page.

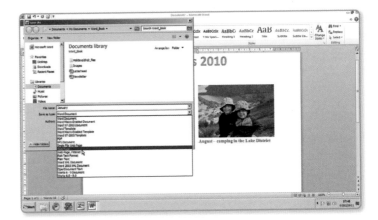

3. When you've finished creating your web page in Word, save it as a Word

Above: When saving the document, change the file type to a web page to enable it to be opened using a web browser such as Internet Explorer.

document (this will make it easier to edit in the future), then save it again as a web page. Press F12 on the keyboard and the Save As dialogue box will appear. Change the file type to Web Page. Make a note of where the web page has been saved.

4. Close or minimize Word and open My Documents, Windows Explorer or Documents Library. Locate the web page you've created in Word. The web page will be saved as a HTML file and there will be a folder of the same name as the web page (with the word '_files' added to the end of the name), which contains any images used in it and additional information. Try opening the HTML file to see if the web page appears in your web browser.

5. If you want to move the web page to a website or to a different location on your computer, then the HTML file and the folder outlined in the last step must be moved together. This will ensure the web page can be opened.

Hot Tip

Press Ctrl+N on the keyboard in Word to start a new blank document.

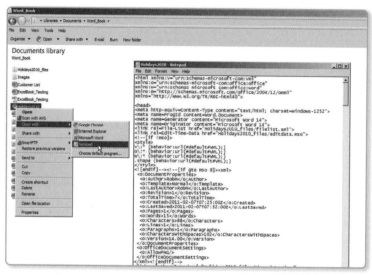

Above: The information (HTML code) behind a web page can be viewed and changed using a program such as Notepad. Right click on the web page, select Open With and choose Notepad from the sub-menu.

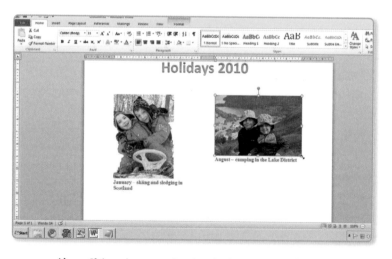

Above: If the web page needs to be edited, open its original Word document and make any changes, then resave it as a web page.

6. The code that has been used to create the web page can be viewed and edited using a program called Notepad. Right click on the HTML file that represents the web page, choose Open With and from the sub-menu that appears, select Notepad. The code will be listed down the page in Notepad and will probably be very long.

7. If you want to make a few changes to the web page (change the text, add more images), then it's often easier to reopen the Word document that was saved in step 3. This will be easier to open in Word and much easier to amend. Resave the web page, overwriting the original, or save it with another name.

WRITE A CV

Word's range of tools and additional features can help to produce a professional-looking curriculum vitae for job applications. The following step-by-step guide shows how to insert headings, sub-headings, tables and a table of contents.

1. Starting with a new or existing document in Word, decide on the structure and the main headings for your CV. For example, there could be a series of headings starting with personal details, followed by qualifications, work experience and finishing with hobbies and interests.

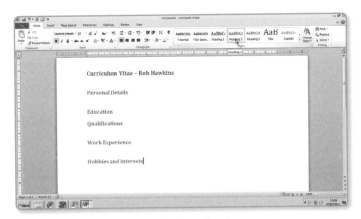

Above: Create the main headings in the CV and apply heading levels to them.

2. Write the main headings for each section of the CV. This will help to organize the structure of the CV and if you want to add or change any of these headings, they can be changed at any point during or after the creation of the document.

3. We're going to apply heading levels to all the headings in the CV. This will assist anyone who reads the CV using Microsoft Word and can also be used to create a contents table. Position the cursor inside a main heading, then choose Heading 1 from the Formatting toolbar or the Home ribbon tab.

4. Where a sub-heading exists (for example, a particular job under the Work Experience heading), use Heading 2. If there's another sub-heading within this section, use Heading 3. Heading levels look professional and make it easier to understand a document.

Above: Some information can be better presented in a table format. Word can quickly insert a table and its style can be changed.

5. Some information in the CV may be easier to understand if it's presented in a table. Hobbies and interests, for example, could be displayed in a simple table with a few columns to allow a brief description of each hobby or interest and another column for any achievements.

6. Depending on the version of Word, a table can be inserted by clicking on the Table menu and choosing Insert, or clicking on the Insert ribbon tab, selecting Table and choosing Insert Table.

Above: If a CV is long, it may be easier to understand if a table of contents is added at the beginning of it.

In all cases, a dialogue box will appear, allowing you to choose the number of rows and columns to use in the table.

7. If the CV is very long, it may be worthwhile inserting a table of contents (TOC) at the beginning of the document. This is covered in more depth in chapter three.

Hot Tip

Select some text to apply a heading to, then hold down the Ctrl and Alt keys and press 1 to apply Heading 1, 2 to apply Heading 2 or 3 to apply Heading 3.

8. If the CV needs to be printed, add headers and footers to include page numbers and your name. Click on the Insert ribbon tab and choose the Header or Footer button in Word 2007–2010, or in Word pre-2007 click on the View menu and choose Header and Footer.

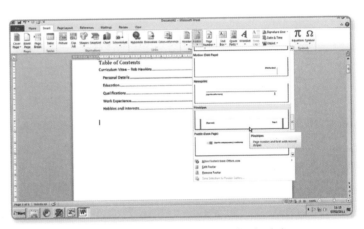

Above: Add a header and footer if the CV will be printed and include information such as page numbers, total number of pages and your name.

FURTHER INFORMATION IN THIS BOOK

Headers and footers: Chapter 2, pages 85–86

Headings: Chapter 3, pages 90–92

Inserting a table of contents: Chapter 3, pages 93–94

Tables: Chapter 3, pages 99–102

LEAFLETS AND POSTERS

Word can produce anything from a 'for sale' notice to an advertisement for a school fête using a variety of different-sized paper. WordArt, page borders, images and photographs can all be added to help illustrate the document.

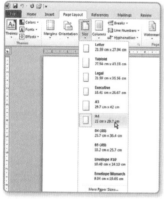

Above: Click on the Page Layout ribbon tab in Word 2007–2010 and use the buttons in the top-left corner of the screen to change the shape and orientation of the page.

1. Open Microsoft Word and start with a new blank document (press Ctrl+N to create a new document). Before starting to create a poster or leaflet, determine the size of it. Word will usually produce an A4 page as standard, which is portrait-orientated. If this needs to be changed, click on the Page Layout ribbon tab in Word 2007–2010 and select the Orientation button to switch to landscape, or click on the Size button to change the page dimensions.

2. In Word pre-2007, the size of the page is changed by clicking on the File menu and choosing Page Setup. From the dialogue box that appears, click on the Paper tab and change the settings underneath Paper size. If the orientation needs changing, this is found under the Margins tab.

Above: The shape and orientation of the page can be changed in Word pre-2007 by clicking on the File menu and choosing Page Setup.

3. A colourful border can be added around the entire page to help illustrate the leaflet or poster. In Word pre-2007, click on the Format menu and choose Borders and Shading. In Word 2007–2010, click on the Page

Layout ribbon tab and select the Page Borders button. In both cases, a Borders and Shading dialogue box will appear. Select the Page Border tab, then choose a type of border, a style, colour and width. Click on OK to return to the document.

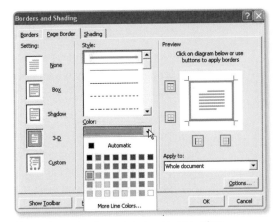

Above: A page border can help to add some colour to a leaflet or poster.

4. Create an eye-catching heading for the leaflet or poster using WordArt. In Word pre-2007, click on the Insert menu, choose Picture and select WordArt from the sub-menu. In later versions of Word, click on the Insert ribbon tab and click on the WordArt button. In both cases a palette of WordArt styles will appear in a dialogue box or drop-down menu. Choose a WordArt style (then click on OK in Word pre-2007), then type the text for the WordArt title and click on OK.

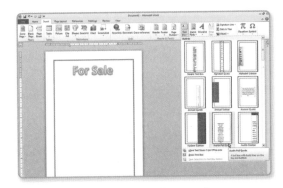

Above: A choice of text boxes can be inserted in Word 2007–2010.

5. Text can be typed on the page and its font and colour changed. However, it may be useful to create some text boxes, where information such as contact details or a list of events can be displayed separately. Click on the Insert menu or ribbon tab and select Text Box. In Word 2007–2010, a choice of text box styles will appear, whereas in earlier versions, a standard text box has to be drawn on the screen.

6. Type the text inside the text box and move the box in the same manner as dragging and dropping an object (position the mouse pointer over the edges of the box). The box can

also be resized by selecting it and positioning the mouse pointer over the small squares or circles around it. When the mouse pointer changes to a double-headed arrow, hold the left button down and move the mouse to resize the box.

7. Images including Clip Art and photos can be added to the page. Click on the Insert menu in Word pre-2007, choose Picture and select From File or Clip Art. In Word 2007–2010, click on the Insert ribbon tab and select the Picture button or the Clip Art button. After locating an image and inserting it, the size of it may be too big or too small. It can be resized in the same way a text box is resized.

Above: Images can be added to a leaflet or poster and resized and moved to a different position.

8. Save the document and, when you're ready to print it, check everything is correctly positioned using Print Preview. In Word pre-2007, click on the File menu and choose Print Preview. In later versions of Word, press Ctrl+F2 on the keyboard.

Above: Print Preview can be used to check a poster or leaflet before printing it.

Hot Tip

A page border can be removed by returning to the Borders and Shading dialogue box and selecting None in the top-left corner of the box under the Page Border tab.

FURTHER INFORMATION IN THIS BOOK

Page border: Chapter 3, pages 110–111
Adding Images: Chapter 3, pages 106–108
WordArt: Chapter 3, pages 107–108
Printing: Chapter 2, pages 83–87

INVITATIONS

Invitations for parties, weddings and other social occasions can be professionally created in Word and printed. The following step-by-step guide shows how to choose the size of an invitation, add images, colour and pictures, and print it out.

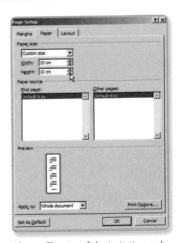

1. Open Microsoft Word and start with a new blank document (press Ctrl+N to create a new document). Decide upon the size of the invitation. Word will usually produce an A4 page as standard, which is portrait-orientated. However, it may be better to produce an A5 (half the size of A4) invitation and print two on one page. Click on the Page Layout ribbon tab in Word 2007–2010 and select the Size button to change the page dimensions (choose More Paper Sizes if the size you want isn't listed).

2. In Word pre-2007, the size of the page is changed by clicking on the File menu and choosing Page Setup. From the dialogue box that appears, click on the Paper tab and change the settings underneath Paper size. In all cases, if the size cannot be found, try selecting a custom size and entering the required dimensions.

Above: The size of the invitation and the space between the edge of the text and the edge of the paper (margins) can all be changed in the Page Setup dialogue box.

3. If the orientation of the page needs to be changed, it can be changed on the Page Layout ribbon tab in Word 2007–2010, or by returning to the Page Setup dialogue box in earlier versions of Word (select Margins tab and look for the Portrait and Landscape options).

4. The margins used in an invitation may be too large, leaving little space to display text. These can be altered by opening the Page Setup dialogue box and altering the Top, Left,

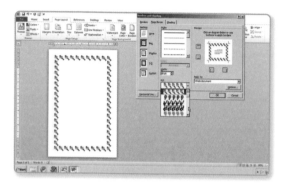

Above: A colourful and artistic border can be added to the invitation.

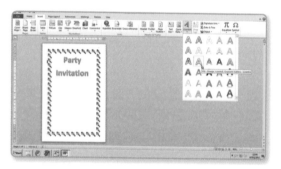

Above: Use WordArt to create a title that stands out for the invitation.

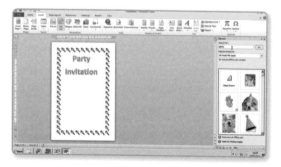

Above: Clip Art relating to the type of invitation can often be found in Word and inserted on to the page.

Bottom and Right values on the Margins tab. This dialogue box is opened in Word pre-2007 by clicking on the File menu and choosing Page Setup. In later versions, click on the Page Layout ribbon tab, then select the Margins button and choose Custom Margins.

5. A colourful border can be added around the entire page to help brighten up the invitation. In Word pre-2007, click on the Format menu and choose Borders and Shading. In Word 2007–2010, click on the Page Layout ribbon tab and select the Page Borders button. In both cases, a Borders and Shading dialogue box will appear. Select the Page Border tab, then choose a type of border, a style, colour and width. Click on OK to return to the invitation.

6. Use WordArt to create an eye-catching title for the invitation. In Word pre-2007, click on the Insert menu, choose Picture and select WordArt from the sub-menu. In later versions of Word, click on the Insert ribbon tab and select the WordArt button. In both cases a palette of WordArt styles will appear in a dialogue box or drop-down menu. Choose a WordArt style (then click on OK in Word pre-2007), then type the text for the WordArt title and click on OK.

7. Add some Clip Art or photos by clicking on the Insert menu in Word pre-2007, choosing Picture and selecting From File or Clip Art. In Word 2007–2010, click on the Insert ribbon tab and select the Picture button or the Clip Art button. Locate and insert an image (*see* bottom picture opposite).

8. Type any text in the page and change the font and colours used to make sure it looks colourful and artistic. Save the document with a meaningful name and double-check there are no spelling or grammatical mistakes.

9. Switch to Print Preview to check how the invitation will look when printed: click on the File menu and choose Print Preview in Word pre-2007 or press Ctrl+F2 in later versions. Before proceeding to print, the number of copies printed on one page can be altered in the Print dialogue box or screen. For example, this might be used to print two A5 invitations on one A4 page.

Above: Check the spelling and grammar before printing the invitation.

Above: Multiple copies can be printed on one sheet, enabling an A5 invitation to be printed twice on a sheet of A4 paper.

Hot Tip

If the ruler is displayed on the screen, double-click on the vertical ruler to open the Page Setup dialogue box and change the size of the page.

CONVERT TO PDF (WORD 2007-2010)

A Word document can be saved as a PDF (portable document format) in Word 2007–2010, making it safer to send to other people and allowing them to read it but not change it. The following step-by-step guide can be applied to Word 2007–2010.

1. Make sure you have Adobe Reader installed on your computer. This can be downloaded for free at http://get.adobe.com/uk/reader. You may need to disable your antivirus software to download the program.

2. With the document you want to convert to PDF open in Word and on the screen, click on the File Ribbon tab or Office button and choose Save As (or press F12 on the keyboard). A Save As dialogue box will appear.

Above: Adobe Reader is used to open a PDF and can be downloaded via the Internet for free.

3. With the Save As dialogue box on screen, look at the option at the bottom of it (under Save as type) and click on the drop-down list of file types. Choose PDF from the list. If you want to change

Right: Open the Save As dialogue box and change the file type to PDF to convert a Word document to a PDF.

the filename for the PDF, click inside the box and type a new name. Also, you can save it to a different location.

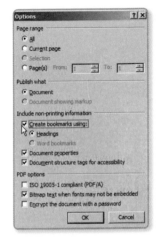

4. Upon choosing to save a file as a PDF, an Options button will appear in the Save As dialogue box. Click on this and another dialogue box will appear with options to convert the entire document or only one page to a PDF and to set a password. Click on OK to return to the Save As dialogue box.

5. If a password was set in the last step, then a dialogue box will appear, requesting a password to be entered. This will be requested whenever the PDF is opened and will help to restrict how the document can be used.

Above: An entire document or specific pages in it can be converted to a PDF.

6. When you're ready to save the PDF, add a tick mark to the option labelled Open file after publishing. Click on the Save button and if a password was set, you will be asked to enter it again before Adobe Reader opens with the converted PDF.

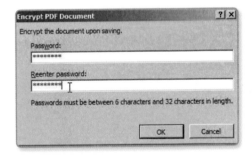

7. Scroll down the PDF to make sure all of the pages from the document have been converted. There is also a Pages button on the left edge of the screen, which provides a thumbnail view of all the pages in the document.

Above: A PDF can be password-protected, requiring a password to be entered whenever the document is opened.

8. A PDF is a more secure method of sending a document to another person or several people and making sure they don't delete or change its contents. It's also a recognized file format which can be opened in software that is available for free. Unfortunately, once a PDF has been created, it can't be reopened in Word, so make sure you keep a .doc copy as well.

CREATE A REUSABLE EXPENSES CLAIM FORM

Create an expenses form that is quick to complete and will automatically calculate any total figures. The following step-by-step guide shows how to insert tables, add up columns of numbers and save a file as a template to use again.

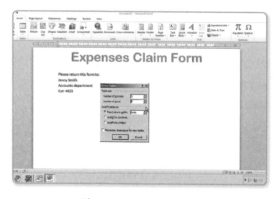

Above: A table can be added to the expenses form to allow expenditure amounts to be totalled.

1. Open Microsoft Word and start with a new blank document (press Ctrl+N if you need to create a new document). Type a title across the top (for example, Expenses) and some personal or expenses-related information below (for example, the name of the person to whom to send the form in order to claim back the expenses).

2. A table can be created, which can be used to enter the expenditure amounts and calculate the total amount that needs to be claimed. In Word pre-2007, click on the Table menu and choose Insert, then select Table from the sub-menu. In Word 2007–2010, click on the Insert ribbon tab, select the Table button and choose Insert Table from the menu. In all cases, a dialogue box will appear.

3. Decide upon the number of rows and columns required to display all the details concerning expenditure and amounts to be claimed. Alter the values in the Insert Table dialogue box, then click on OK and a table will appear in the document.

4. Enter some information into the table relating to expenditure. Don't enter any specific information yet. This will be done when the form is used (a general expenses claim form has to be created first). The table can be resized and colours changed using the Tables and Borders toolbar or the Design and Layout ribbon tabs when the table is selected.

Above: The layout and presentation of the table used in the expenses claim form can be changed.

5. Enter zero values (the number 0) in the column where amounts need to be entered. At the bottom of this column, a total calculation can be entered, which will add up the numbers above. Click inside the cell where the total figure will be displayed. In Word 2007–2010, click on the Layout ribbon tab, then select the Formula button (top-right corner of the screen). In earlier versions of Word, click on the Table menu and select Formula.

6. After selecting Formula from the Table menu or Layout ribbon tab, a dialogue box will appear. Make sure the words =SUM(ABOVE) are displayed underneath Formula. Choose a number format, then click on OK. Check this calculation works by changing one of the amounts, then right click on the total calculation and choose Update Field.

7. The structure of the expenses form has now been created. Save the file as a template (change the file type to template when saving it). When the document needs to be used again, click on File (the Office button in Word 2007) and choose New to locate the template. This will safeguard the original document.

FURTHER INFORMATION IN THIS BOOK

Tables: Chapter 3, pages 99–102
Templates: Chapter 2, pages 36–57

LETTERHEADS

Create a document with your address displayed at the top, which can be used again and again without destroying the original. The following step-by-step guide shows how to insert your address and allocate an adjacent space for the recipient's address, include a date that automatically updates and save the document as a template.

1. A letterhead that can be used several times for different letters should only contain text and images (for example, a company logo) that appear in every letter. For example, your address, a greeting line such as Dear and a closing sentence followed by Yours sincerely and your name might always appear in a letter. This can be included in a letterhead, which will be saved as a template and used as many times as required.

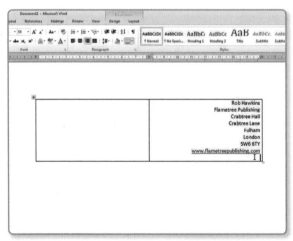

Above: Type your address details inside the right-hand cell of the table. Its height will increase as additional lines of the address are entered.

2. Starting with a blank document (press Ctrl+N to open a new blank document), enter your address details on the right-hand side of the page (click on the Align Text Right button on the Formatting toolbar or Home ribbon tab). However, if you want the recipient's address details to appear to the left of your address, then both addresses should be displayed in a table (see the next step on creating a table).

3. If your address and the recipient's address need to be displayed side by side in the letterhead, then the first step is to insert a table with two columns and one row. In Word pre-2007, click on the Table menu, choose Insert and select Table. In Word 2007–2010, click on the Insert ribbon tab, select Table and choose Insert Table. In both cases, a dialogue box will appear. Change the row and column numbers to one row and two columns, then click on OK.

Above: If your address and the recipient's address need to be displayed side by side, first create a table consisting of two columns and one row.

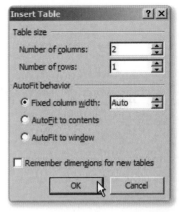

4. With the table displayed in the document, click inside the right-hand side cell, change the alignment to right and enter your address (press Return on the keyboard to move down a line). The height of the table will grow as the address is typed. Don't worry about the table's black borders. These will be removed in the next step.

Above: Remove the colour from the border of the table to ensure it won't appear when a letter is printed.

5. After entering your address details inside the right side of the table, the border for the table can now be removed so that it won't appear when a letter is created and printed. Click inside the table and a small cross should appear above the top-left corner of it. Click on this cross and the entire table will be selected. In Word 2007–2010, click on the Design ribbon tab, select the Borders button

Above: In Word pre-2007, a border is removed from a table using the Borders button on the Formatting toolbar or the Tables and Borders toolbar.

Hot Tip

If a toolbar is missing in Word pre-2007, right click on any toolbar button and a checklist of toolbars will appear. Select the toolbar you need and it will appear on the screen.

and choose No Border. In earlier versions of Word, select the table in the same manner, but click on the Borders toolbar button on the Formatting toolbar or the Tables and Borders toolbar, then select No Border from the palette of border styles.

6. If you want to add a logo to your letterhead, position the cursor at the point where the image should be located, then click on the Insert menu or ribbon tab (Word 2007–2010), choose Picture and, in Word pre-2007, select From File. A dialogue box will appear enabling you to locate and insert an image, such as a logo.

Above: A logo can be inserted into a letterhead as a picture image.

7. If the logo needs to be resized, select it and a series of circles or squares will appear around it. Position the mouse pointer over one of these circles or squares and when the mouse pointer changes to a double-headed arrow, hold the left button down and move the mouse to resize the image.

Above: An image such as a logo can be aligned in the same way as text using the Formatting toolbar buttons in Word pre-2007 or the buttons on the Home ribbon tab in Word 2007–2010.

8. A date can be inserted below your address, and that date automatically updates whenever a new letterhead is created. Move to the point in the document where the date will be displayed (click on the right-align button to display the date on the right side of the

page). Click on the Insert menu or ribbon tab and select Date and Time. From the dialogue box that appears, select a date format and add a tick mark to the option labelled Update automatically. Click on OK to add a date to your letterhead.

9. Type some standard text that is often used in a letter. For example, an opening word, such as Dear, or an opening sentence, such as 'I refer to our telephone conversation'. Add a closing sentence, the words Yours sincerely, and your name and any relevant contact details (email address, direct line phone number).

10. Save the document as a template: in the Save As dialogue box, change the file type to a template. This will allow the letterhead to be used again and again without destroying the original. When you need to use the letterhead in Word, click on the File menu or ribbon tab (the Office button in Word 2007) and choose New, then locate the letterhead template.

Above: A date that is automatically updated can be entered into a letterhead .

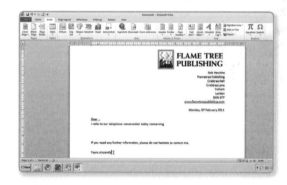

Above: Repetitive words and sentences that are used in most letters can be entered in the letterhead to help save time when typing.

Hot Tip

If a table is at the top of a document and you want to insert something above it, click inside the top left cell and press Return. The table will move down one line in the document.

NEWSLETTERS

Word can help create newsletters for clubs, churches and social groups, and it's a lot easier than using a desktop publishing program. The following step-by-step guide covers choosing the paper size, adding borders, WordArt and Clip Art, writing text and printing a newsletter.

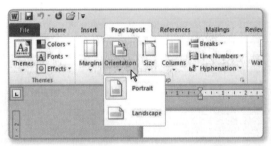

Above: Decide how the newsletter is going to be arranged before writing it.

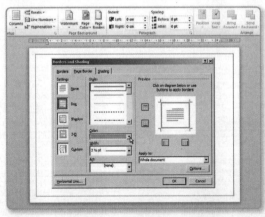

Above: A page border can add some colour to a newsletter.

1. Decide on the page layout of the newsletter and how it will be printed or photocopied. For example, if the newsletter uses A5-size pages, but is printed on two sides of an A4 piece of paper, you may want to set up the page as A4 landscape, then divide it into two A5 pages.

2. The page set-up of the newsletter can be changed by clicking on the File menu in Word pre-2007 and choosing Page Setup. From the dialogue box that appears, there are settings for margins, paper size and orientation. In Word 2007–2010, click on the Page Layout ribbon tab and select the buttons for Margins, Orientation and Size.

3. A colourful border can be added around the entire page to help brighten up the newsletter. In Word pre-2007, click on the Format menu and choose Borders and Shading. In Word

2007–2010, click on the Page Layout ribbon tab and select the Page Borders button. In both cases, a Borders and Shading dialogue box will appear. Select the Page Border tab, then choose a type of border, a style, colour and width. Click on OK to return to the newsletter.

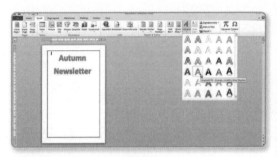

Above: WordArt can be used to create an artistic heading for a newsletter.

4. Use WordArt to create an eye-catching title for the newsletter. In Word pre-2007, click on the Insert menu, choose Picture and select WordArt from the sub-menu. In later versions of Word, click on the Insert ribbon tab and select the WordArt button. In both cases a palette of WordArt styles will appear in a dialogue box or drop-down menu. Choose a WordArt style (then click on OK in Word pre-2007), then type the text for the WordArt title and click on OK.

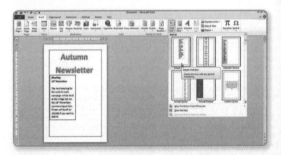

Above: Text boxes are useful for creating an article in a box in a column style.

5. If your newsletter contains several short news items, you may find it easier to display each news item inside a text box. Click on the Insert menu or ribbon tab and choose Text Box. Depending on the version of Word, you will have to either choose a style of Text box or draw one on the page. You can then write your text inside the text box.

Above: A text box or image can be resized by positioning the mouse pointer over the circles around it, as shown here. When the pointer changes to a double-headed arrow, hold the left button down and move the mouse to resize the object.

6. If the text box needs to be resized, make sure it's selected, then position the mouse

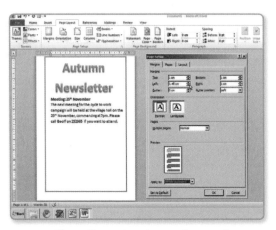

Above: Text can be written on the page of a newsletter, but if the border gets in the way, the margins will need to be adjusted.

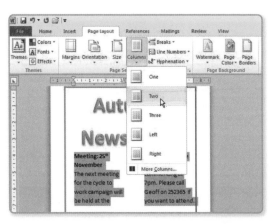

Above: Text written on the page of a newsletter can be displayed in columns, just like a newspaper.

pointer over one of the circles or squares around it. When the mouse pointer changes to a double-headed arrow, hold the left button down and move the mouse to resize it (release the left button to stop resizing). Use the circles or squares at the edges of the text box to resize the height and width of the text box.

7. If the text box needs to be moved, make sure it is selected, then position the mouse pointer on the edge of it, away from any of the circles or squares around it, which are used for resizing. When the mouse pointer adopts a cross with arrows, hold the left button down and move the mouse pointer to move the text box. Release the left button to stop moving the text box.

8. Whilst text boxes are useful for creating a newsletter containing several news items, if your newsletter contains only one or two articles, then it may be easier simply to write the text on the page. If a border has been added, this may get in the way of the text, so you will need to adjust the margins (see step 2).

9. Another approach to displaying text in a newsletter is to use two or more columns. The text has to be written on the page (not in a text box) and the columns can be chosen before or after it has been written (select the text if it has been written). Click on the Page

Layout ribbon tab in Word 2007–2010, select the Columns button and choose the number of columns. In earlier versions of Word, click on the Format menu, choose Columns and, from the dialogue box that appears, set the value for the number of columns before clicking on OK.

Above: Word has a vast assortment of templates, including several designs of newsletter.

10. Add some Clip Art or photos to the newsletter by clicking on the Insert menu in Word pre-2007, choosing Picture and selecting From File or Clip Art. In Word 2007–2010, click on the Insert ribbon tab and select the Picture button or the Clip Art button. After locating an image and inserting it, the size of it may be too big or too small. It can be resized in the same way a text box is resized.

11. Save the document and, when you're ready to print the newsletter, use the Print Preview screen to check it first (click on the File menu and choose Print Preview in Word pre-2007, or press Ctrl+F2 in later versions).

12. An alternative method of creating a newsletter is to use a template. Most versions of Word have a range of newsletter templates, which contain artwork and sections to enter text. Click on the File menu (Office button in Word 2007) and choose New. Look for the templates and search through them to find a newsletter.

FURTHER INFORMATION IN THIS BOOK

Printing: Chapter 2, pages 83–87
Columns: Chapter 3, pages 103–104
Page border: Chapter 3, pages 110–111
Adding Images: Chapter 3, pages 106–108
WordArt: Chapter 3, pages 107–108

WRITE A REPORT

A report for a college assignment or work can be quickly created in Word and made to look organized and professional. The following step-by-step guide shows how to apply heading levels, insert footnotes and endnotes, add page numbers, display headers and footers, and create a contents page.

Above: Start a report by creating the main headings and allocating heading levels (for example, Heading 1, Heading 2).

Above: A chart can often illustrate information more clearly than text. Word can create charts, which can be included in a report.

1. Create the headings for the report. Most reports include an introduction, aims and objectives, a summary, results and a conclusion. More headings can be added at any point, but it's good practice to start a report by creating its structure.

2. Convert any headings to a heading level. For example, a main heading, such as the introduction, can be classed as Heading 1 (the top-level heading). To set a heading such as Heading 1, position the cursor inside the heading (you don't need to select the heading), then select Heading 1 from the Formatting toolbar in Word pre-2007 or the Home ribbon tab in Word 2007–2010.

3. Once the headings have been created, you can start to write the report. Where possible, try to present information in an easy-to-understand format. For example, sales results

could be displayed in a table or chart. These subjects were covered in chapter three.

4. Whenever some information in the report needs a point of reference or a further explanation, this can be added as a footnote at the bottom of the page. Select the last word in the text that requires the footnote. In Word 2007–2010, click on the References ribbon tab and select the Insert Footnote button. A number will appear next to the selected text and the same number will be displayed at the bottom of the page. Type some text for the footnote at the bottom of the page, then click back into the document to continue typing the report.

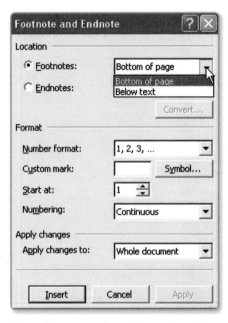

Above: Footnotes can be used to provide a reference or further information concerning a point in a report.

5. In Word pre-2007, select the last word in the text that requires a footnote, then click on the Insert menu, select Footnote, or Reference followed by Footnote from the sub-menu. A dialogue box will appear with a choice of formatting for the footnote. Select any relevant options, then click on Insert and the dialogue box will close. Type the text for the footnote, then click back into the document to continue typing the report.

6. Add page numbers to the report by clicking on the Insert menu or ribbon tab and selecting Page Number(s). A menu of page number options will appear in Word 2007–2010, whereas a dialogue box will appear in earlier versions of the program.

Hot Tip

Press Ctrl+Home to jump to the start of a document and press Ctrl+End to jump to the end of a document.

Above: A table of contents helps to show where specific headings are in a report. Word can quickly create a table of contents, providing headings have been used in the report (for example, Heading 1, Heading 2, Heading 3).

7. Headers and footers can be used to display information, including the version of the report, the date it was printed, page numbers and total number of pages. Click on the View menu in Word pre-2007 and choose Header and Footer to add information to the top and bottom of each page. In Word 2007–2010, click on the Insert ribbon tab and select either the Header or Footer button for a choice of options.

8. A table of contents can be inserted at the beginning of the report to show where the main headings can be found. Position the cursor at the point in the document where the table of contents (TOC) needs to be created. You may want to add a blank page, so press Ctrl+Enter on the keyboard.

9. To add a table of contents in Word 2007–2010, click on the References ribbon tab and select the Table of Contents button (top-left corner of the screen). A list of TOC styles will appear. Choose one of them and a table of contents will appear in the document.

10. To add a table of contents in Word pre-2007, click on the Insert menu, choose Index and Tables, or Reference followed by Index and Tables. An Index and Tables dialogue box will appear. Select the Table of Contents tab, then choose a style for the TOC and check the

Hot Tip
The numbers used for footnotes are automatically changed if more footnotes are inserted into a document.

settings are correct. Click on OK to create the table of contents in the document.

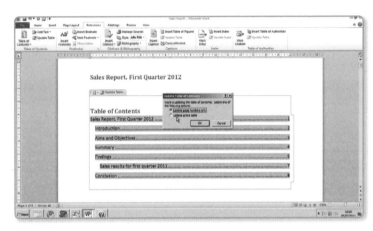

11. The table of contents can be used to jump to particular headings in the report. Position the mouse over a heading in the table of contents, then hold down the Ctrl key on the keyboard and left click on the heading to jump to it.

Above: As the report grows, the table of contents will need to be updated. Right click inside it and choose Update Field.

12. As the report grows or is edited, the table of contents may need updating. Right click on it and choose Update Field. Select either to update the entire table or to update the page numbers. Word will check the headings and page numbers in the report and amend the table of contents accordingly.

Hot Tip

Select some text to which to apply a heading, then hold down the Ctrl and Alt keys and press 1 to apply Heading 1, 2 to apply Heading 2 or 3 to apply Heading 3.

FURTHER INFORMATION IN THIS BOOK

Headings: Chapter 3, pages 90–92
Inserting a table of contents: Chapter 3, pages 93–94
Creating a chart: Chapter 3, pages 113–116
Footnotes: Chapter 6, pages 230–232

PLAN A HOLIDAY

Word can be used to compare offers, calculate prices and organize checklists for a holiday. The following pages cover using a table to list prices and packages, and creating a checklist.

HOLIDAY DILEMMAS

Planning a holiday usually results in several choices with several prices to consider. The decision isn't always based on price: flight times, distance, dates, location and extras can all influence which holiday is selected. However, choosing a holiday can turn into a minefield of information, so Word can be used to organize this information and help make a rational decision.

Above: Word can be used to organize holiday details in a table.

TABLE THE DATA

A table in a Word document can be used to list important information concerning a holiday, such as flight departure and arrival dates and times, prices for flights, transfers, car hire, accommodation and extras. Insert a table for each holiday and organize this information into a table. To insert a table, click on the Table menu in Word pre-2007 and choose Insert followed by Table from the sub-menu. In Word 2007–2010, click on the Insert ribbon tab, select the Table button and choose Insert Table. In both cases, a dialogue box will appear. Enter the number of rows and columns for the table and click on OK.

Sort a Column

If the items listed in a table need to be sorted, position the cursor inside the table, then click on the Insert menu and choose Sort, in Word pre-2007, or in Word 2007–2010, click on the Layout ribbon tab and select the Sort button. In all cases, a Sort dialogue box will appear. If the table has a header row (titles across the top), make sure this option is selected to avoid sorting the headings. Choose the column to sort and whether it's ascending or descending, then click on OK. If a Total row is at the bottom of the table, this will also be sorted.

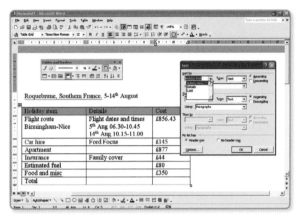

Above: Information displayed in a table can be sorted to help organize it and make it easier to understand.

Total a Column

One of the most important considerations for a holiday is the total cost of it. If the costs are listed in a column inside a table, a total figure can be displayed at the bottom. Word can add up a column of numbers, but make sure there are no empty cells in the column, otherwise Word cannot add up all the numbers.

Insert a Formula

Position the cursor in the first empty cell below the column of numbers. Click on the Table menu in Word pre-2007 and choose Formula, or in Word 2007–2010, click on the Layout ribbon tab and select the formula button. From the dialogue box that appears, make sure the formula =SUM(ABOVE) is displayed in the top box, underneath Formula. If it isn't, write this formula in the box. Choose a number format for the total, then click on OK.

Above: Once you've listed all the costs involved in a holiday inside a table, these values can be totalled.

Update the Total

If any of the costs are changed in the table, then the total calculation outlined in the previous section will not automatically update itself. Instead, right click on the formula for the total and choose Update Field to recalculate the total.

CREATE A CHECKLIST

A checklist of what to take on holiday (passports, insurance certificate, driving licence, flip-flops, goggles) can help with packing and making sure you haven't forgotten anything. This can begin as a simple numbered list, but Word can help to cross off things, highlight anything important and sort the list.

Create a Numbered List with Sub-Points

A numbered list detailing everything to take on holiday could result in pages of unorganized items, but a numbered list with sub-points can be very useful. Start by creating a normal numbered list, typing the number 1 and a full stop, followed by a couple of spaces, then type some words for a category of items (for example, documents, clothes). Press Return on the keyboard and Word will start a numbered list and automatically enter a number 2 below. However, press the Tab key on the keyboard and the number 2 will be changed to a sub-point (the cursor must be at the beginning of the line and to the right of the number).

Switching Using Tab and Shift+Tab

Whilst the Tab key changes a point in a numbered list to a sub-point, pressing Shift+Tab moves it back a level (the cursor must be at the beginning of the line and to the right of the number). This is known as promoting and demoting. It can help to create an organized checklist and make sure you don't forget anything.

Cross It Off

Items in a checklist can be crossed off using the Strikethrough feature. Select the text to be crossed off, then press Ctrl+D on the keyboard. The font dialogue box will appear. Add a tick mark to the option for Strikethrough or Double strikethrough, then click on OK.

CREATE A QUESTIONNAIRE

A questionnaire with tick boxes, options lists and comments can be created and completed in Word. The following pages cover creating tables, numbered lists, adding tick boxes and saving a questionnaire as a secure document.

COMPLETE ONLINE OR PRINT IT OUT

A questionnaire can be created in Word, but it can either be printed out for people to complete, or emailed to various people for them to complete using Word.

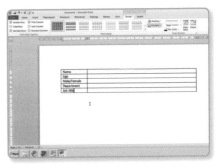

Above: A table can be used to organise information required for a questionnaire.

TABLES IN QUESTIONNAIRES

Questions contained in a questionnaire need to be displayed in an organized and structured manner. It may help to insert a table with one column for the questions and a second column for the answers. A table can be created in Word by clicking on the Insert ribbon tab in Word 2007–2010, selecting the Table button and choosing Insert Table from the drop-down menu. In earlier versions of Word, click on the Table menu, select Insert and choose Table. In all cases, a dialogue box will appear; select the number of rows and columns for the table, then click on OK.

NUMBERED LISTS

Questions in a questionnaire can be displayed in a numbered list. Start a numbered list by typing the number (and a full stop) followed by a couple of spaces, then the text. Press Return on the keyboard after typing the text and the next number will automatically appear.

QUESTIONNAIRE FORM BUTTONS

Word can insert tick boxes, drop-down lists and other useful options for helping to produce a professional-looking questionnaire. These features are called form buttons or control buttons.

Above: Word 2007–2010 uses an additional Developer ribbon tab for creating a questionnaire, which has to be added to the main screen.

Find the Control Buttons in Word 2007-2010

Click on the File menu or Office button and select Word Options or Options. From the dialogue box that appears, select Customize Ribbon from the list on the left. Click on the top-left drop-down arrow underneath Choose commands from and select Main Tabs from the list. The list underneath will change to the main ribbon tabs used in Word. Select Developer from this list, then click on the Add button in the middle of the dialogue box. Click on OK to return to the Word screen. The Developer ribbon tab should be displayed along the top of the screen. Click on it to see the buttons that accompany it.

Find the Form Buttons in Word Pre-2007

Right click on any toolbar button and a checklist of toolbars will appear. Select Forms from the checklist and a Forms toolbar will appear with a number of useful buttons to help create a questionnaire.

TICK BOXES

Tick boxes (called check boxes) can be used to select a specific option, such as male or female, or choose a rating (poor, good, excellent). They can be inserted into a table or displayed on the page. In Word 2007–2010,

Above: Tick boxes can be added to a questionnaire to enable choices to be selected.

select the Developer ribbon tab and click on the Check Box Content Control button, which looks like a white box with a tick mark inside it. In Word pre-2007, there is a Check Box Form Field button on the Forms toolbar, which also looks like a white box with a tick mark inside it.

Modify Tick Boxes

Right click on a tick box in Word pre-2007 and choose Properties to change the settings behind it. In Word 2007–2010, select a tick box and click on the Properties button on the Developer ribbon tab.

DROP-DOWN LISTS

A drop-down list is a useful method of ensuring specific answers are chosen in a questionnaire. The entries in the drop-down list can be created when the questionnaire is being produced.

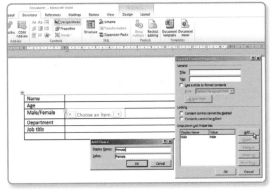

Creating a Drop-Down List in Word 2007–2010

Position the cursor at the point where the drop-down list needs to be displayed. Click on the

Above: The entries for a drop-down list are added using two dialogue boxes in Word 2007–2010.

Developer ribbon tab and select the Drop-Down List Content Control button. A grey box will appear on the page with the words 'Choose an item'. Click on the Properties button and a Content Control Properties dialogue box will appear. Click on the Add button and a smaller dialogue box will appear. Type a word in the top box, which you want to display in the drop-down list. Click on OK to return to the larger dialogue box. Click on Add and repeat this procedure to add all the drop-down list entries. Finally, click on OK to return to the document.

Creating a Drop-Down List in Word Pre-2007

Position the cursor at the point where the drop-down list needs to be displayed. Click on the Drop-Down Form Field button on the Forms toolbar. A small grey rectangle will appear on the page. Right click inside it and choose Properties. A dialogue box will appear on screen. Type an entry in the box in the top-left corner (underneath Drop-down item) to appear in the drop-down list, then click on the Add button. Continue adding entries for the drop-down list, then click on OK to return to the document.

MAKE SPACE FOR TEXT

If controls such as check boxes and drop-down lists are used in a questionnaire, then space may need to be allocated to allow text to be typed. When the questionnaire is being completed, text cannot be typed anywhere in the document, so a control or field needs to be created for typing text. Position the cursor at a point in the questionnaire where text will be typed, then do the following, depending on the version of Word:

↪ **Word 2007–2010:** Click on the Developer ribbon tab and select one of the Aa buttons. The rich text Aa button allows the formatting of the text to be changed, whereas the other plain text Aa button does not. In both cases, a box will appear where the cursor was last positioned, containing the words 'Click here to enter text'.

↪ **Word pre-2007:** Click on the Text Form Field button on the Forms toolbar. A small grey rectangle will appear where the cursor was last positioned. Its size and the type of text entered can be controlled by right clicking inside it and choosing Properties.

TEST THE QUESTIONNAIRE

The questionnaire should be tested before it is distributed to make sure the tick boxes and drop-down lists work properly. This involves restricting the editing of the questionnaire in Word 2007–2010, or protecting the form in Word pre-2007.

Restrict Editing in Word 2007-2010
Click on the Developer ribbon tab in Word 2007–2010 and choose the Restrict Editing button.

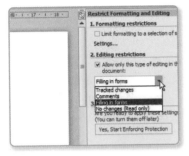

Above: In Word 2007–2010 check boxes and drop-down lists can be protected by restricting the editing of a document.

A task pane, titled Restrict Formatting and Editing, will appear down the right side of the screen. Add a tick mark underneath section two of this task pane (Editing restrictions), then click on the drop-down list below it and choose Filling in forms. Click on the button near the bottom of the task pane, labelled Yes, Start Enforcing Protection. An optional password box will appear before the questionnaire is protected and only the tick boxes, drop-down lists and text boxes can be used. Text cannot be typed elsewhere in the document.

Protect a Questionnaire in Word Pre-2007

Click on the Protect Form button (looks like a padlock) on the Forms toolbar. The document will now be protected and only the tick boxes, drop-down lists and text boxes can be used. Text cannot be typed elsewhere in the document.

Securing the Questionnaire

If the questionnaire is emailed to people or stored on a server or computer that several people can access, the document needs to be secured to make sure the questionnaire can be completed and not changed. In Word 2007–2010, see the section Restrict Editing in Word 2007–2010. In earlier versions of Word, click on the Tools menu and choose Protect Document. From the dialogue box that appears, select the Forms option and enter a password if required.

CREATE A QUESTIONNAIRE TEMPLATE

When the questionnaire is complete and ready to be distributed, you may want to save it as a template to avoid changing the original. To save the document as a template, press F12 on the keyboard and a Save As dialogue box will appear. Change the file type to a template and choose a location to save it. When you want to use a blank copy of the questionnaire, create a new document from this template.

ADVANCED WORD

MAIL MERGE

Mail merge allows names, addresses and other details to be inserted in documents including an invitation, email or Christmas newsletter, to personalize them and save time typing and copying text. The following pages provide an in-depth guide to using mail merge.

SETTING UP A LIST

Word can use contacts from Outlook, a list created in an Access database or Excel, or a list created and stored in Word to create documents with personal information inserted. The list of information used in a mail merge is known as the data source in early versions of Word and the recipients in more recent versions of the program.

Contacts from Outlook

Word can communicate with Outlook and extract the contacts listed in this program. The number of contacts can be refined in Word to include only specific people.

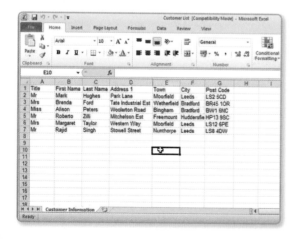

A List in Excel

A list created in Excel can be used by Word to create a mail merge. Ideally, the Excel file should contain one worksheet and the list should start at the top of the sheet with headings across the top and the information listed down the screen. This is the easiest format for Word to understand and use in a mail merge.

Left: A list created in Excel can be used with Word's Mail Merge.

Create a List in Word

A list of names, addresses and other details can be created as a Word document and used with a mail merge.

MAIL MERGE STEPS IN BRIEF

Mail Merge has evolved and changed throughout the different versions of Word, but the general principles of this feature remain the same. There are three parts to a mail merge, which are as follows:

→ **The main document**: The document that will be used in the mail merge. This can be a letter, invitation, labels, an envelope, email message or any other document. Data from a list will be entered into this document to personalize each copy that is produced. The main document is similar to a master document.

→ **Data source or recipients**: The list of names, addresses or other details that will be inserted into each copy of the main document to personalize them. This can be created in Word or another program, or extracted from Outlook's contacts. They can be filtered to ensure only a few are used in the mail merge.

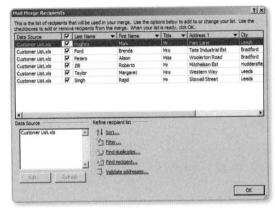

Above: The recipients can be filtered and removed before a mail merge, even if they were created in another program.

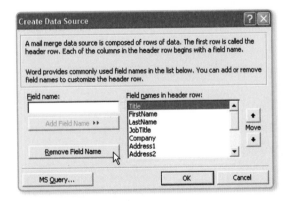

Above: The different categories of information (name, surname) are automatically provided in a mail merge, but can be removed or changed.

➔ **Insert and merge:** The categories from the data source or recipients (name, surname, address) are entered into the main document, then the mail merge produces individual copies of the main document, which contain personal information from each recipient.

Hot Tip

Mail merge is useful for creating emails, sending them to several people and inserting personal information in each one.

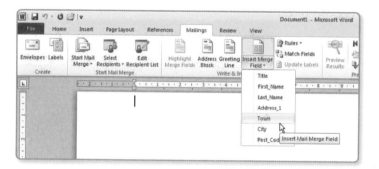

Above: The Mail Merge buttons are on the Mailings ribbon tab in Word 2007–2010.

MAIL MERGE IN WORD 2007-2010

Click on the Mailings ribbon tab and a series of mail merge-related buttons will appear across the top of the screen. If you want to create envelopes or labels for a mail merge, there are specific buttons for these in the top-left corner of the screen. Otherwise, click on the Start Mail Merge button and choose a type of document to create for the mail merge (letter, email). Next, click on the Select Recipients button and choose to type a new list, use an existing list or extract information from contacts in Outlook. In all cases, the recipients can be edited in Word, so specific people can be removed if required.

Adding Fields

Use the Ribbon buttons to add an Address Block, Greeting Line or a Merge Field (name, surname, address). At the same time, the document used in the mail merge can be created and edited. Finally, click on the Finish & Merge button and choose either to edit each document, print them all or send them as email messages.

MAIL MERGE IN WORD 2002–2003

The task pane is used to create a mail merge in Word 2002–2003, which is displayed down the right-hand side of the screen. This runs through a step-by-step guide to mail merging. At each stage, read the information in the task pane, choose any options you want, then click on whatever is displayed in the bottom-right corner of the screen to proceed to the next step.

Starting a Mail Merge in the Task Pane

If you know how to use the task pane, then change the category listed at the top to Mail Merge. If you're not familiar with the task pane, then click on the Tools menu, choose Letters and Mailings, then select Mail Merge Wizard from the sub-menu. In both cases the mail merge will appear down the right-hand side of the screen.

Above: The task pane is used in Word 2002–2003 to produce a mail merge.

Hot Tip

Switch the task pane on and off in Word 2002–2003 by clicking on the View menu and choosing Task Pane.

Six Steps to Mail Merge

There are six steps for mail merging in Word 2002–2003. The stage of the step is detailed in the bottom-right corner of the screen. The first step is to choose the document type (letter, email, envelope), then the document or template to use. Step three chooses the source for the recipients (type a list, Outlook contacts, an existing list), then you can write the main document and insert the categories of information from the recipients (name, surname, address). The final two steps check all the copies that will be created by combining the main document with the information from each recipient before they are printed or emailed.

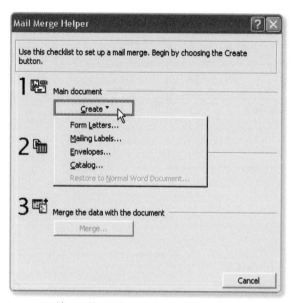

Above: The Mail Merge Helper in Word 2000 and earlier versions provides step-by-step instructions on creating a mail merge.

MAIL MERGE IN WORD PRE-2002

Click on the Tools menu and select Mail Merge. A Mail Merge Helper dialogue box will appear or a Mail Merge Wizard. This consists of the three sections outlined under Mail Merge steps in brief. Each step has to be completed before proceeding to the next. Word can create a list of recipients (a data source), which is saved as a Word document and can be reused in other mail merges. The categories of information for the recipients can be chosen (name, surname, title) and the information is entered in a dialogue box that looks like a form.

Add Fields Using the Mail Merge Toolbar

Once the recipients have been chosen or created, the main document can be edited and the categories of information for the recipients entered. Use the buttons on the Mail Merge toolbar to insert fields (name, surname). Once the main document is finished and all the categories of information are in position, click on the Merge to New Document button to run the mail merge and create copies of the main document with personal information inserted. There will then be at least two documents open: a document called FormLetters1.doc, which will contain all the copies of the main document with personal information inserted, and the original main document (the master copy). Both of these documents can be saved.

Hot Tip

An Address Block helps to save time with correctly laying out an address in a mail merge.

CUSTOMIZING TOOLBARS AND RIBBONS

The toolbar and ribbon buttons can all be modified in Word to help customize the layout of the screen and display the most frequently used tools. The following pages cover adding and removing ribbons, assigning keyboard shortcuts and creating toolbars.

ADDING AND REMOVING RIBBON TABS IN WORD 2007–2010

Click on the File menu or Office button and choose Options or Word Options. From the dialogue box that appears, click on the Customize ribbon option listed on the left. Click on the drop-down list near the top left of the screen, underneath the heading Choose commands from. Select Main Tabs from the list that drops down. Underneath, there will be a list of the main ribbon tabs that can be displayed in the Word screen. On the right-hand side of the dialogue box, the ribbon tabs that are currently displayed will be listed. Use the Add and Remove buttons in the centre of the dialogue box to include or exclude particular ribbon tabs.

ASSIGNING KEYBOARD SHORTCUTS

If you're familiar with using keyboard shortcuts (for example, Ctrl+S to save a document), then you can assign your own keyboard shortcuts to particular commands.

Above: Ribbon tabs can be added and removed from the screen in Word 2007–2010.

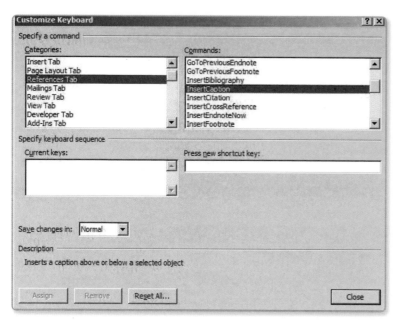

Assigning Keyboard Shortcuts in Word 2007–2010

Click on the File menu or Office button and choose Options or Word Options. From the dialogue box that appears, click on the Customize ribbon option listed on the left. Next, click on the Customize button near the bottom left of the dialogue box. A Customize Keyboard dialogue box will appear on the screen. Select a

Above: If you regularly use particular commands that require several actions to operate, assigning a keyboard shortcut could save time.

category from the list on the left and a particular command from the list on the right. If a shortcut key is assigned for this command, it will be displayed, otherwise click inside the box underneath Press new shortcut key, then assign a new set of keys for it (if these keys have already been used, this will be displayed inside the dialogue box).

Assigning Keyboard Shortcuts in Word Pre-2007

Right click on any toolbar button and choose Customize. From the dialogue box that appears, click on the Keyboard button near the bottom and a second dialogue box will appear. Select a category from the list on the left and a particular command from the list on the right. If a shortcut key is assigned for this command, it will be displayed, otherwise click inside the box underneath Press new shortcut key, then assign a new set of keys for it (if these keys have already been used, this will be displayed inside the dialogue box).

ADDING MENU OPTIONS TO TOOLBARS IN WORD PRE-2007

Right click on any toolbar button and from the shortcut menu that appears, select Customize. A dialogue box will appear. Any menu options within the Commands tab in this dialogue box can be dragged and dropped on to a toolbar on the screen. Once a menu option has been moved into a toolbar, it can be removed by dragging and dropping it back inside the Customize dialogue box.

Hot Tip

When dragging and dropping toolbar buttons, hold down the Ctrl key to copy them instead of moving them.

Hot Tip

If some buttons are missing from a toolbar, open the Customize dialogue box, select the toolbar from the list and click on the Reset button.

CREATE YOUR OWN TOOLBAR IN WORD PRE-2007

Right click on any toolbar button and from the shortcut menu that appears, select Customize. A dialogue box will appear. Select the Toolbars tab and click on the New button. A New Toolbar dialogue box will appear. Enter a name for the toolbar, making sure it is not the same as any other toolbars, then click on OK. The new toolbar will appear on the screen. Drag and drop any existing toolbar buttons into it or any menu options from the Commands tab. Click on the Toolbars tab and select any of the toolbars without tick marks to display them on screen and use their buttons in your toolbar.

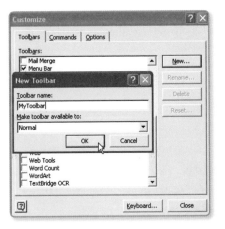

Left: Create your own toolbars in Word pre-2007 and add existing buttons and menu options.

MACROS

A macro is useful for automatically repeating a procedure, such as changing a font and removing bold from copied text. This can save time on selecting buttons and menus options. The following pages show how to create, playback, edit and assign a macro.

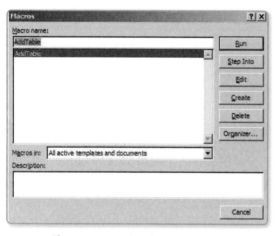

Above: Macros are listed inside a Macros dialogue box. They are automated routines that can help to save time on repetitive tasks.

MACRO EXAMPLES

A macro is similar to recording a number of on-screen actions, then playing them back whenever you need them. In theory, this can be much quicker than having to repeat all of the actions yourself. For example, if you frequently create a table with five rows and columns, and the same headings across the top, then a macro could do this for you. Other examples of macros concern formatting. If text is regularly copied from emails or the Internet and needs to be altered, then a macro can do this instantly.

Macros Versus AutoText

Sometimes, a macro is not necessary. For example, if the opening sentences of a letter are regularly used, then they should be assigned to AutoText, not recorded as a macro.

Macro Limitations

There are a number of operations that cannot be recorded by Word in a macro. You will discover most of these when you find they do not work when attempting to record or play back a macro.

MACRO MENU, RIBBONS AND BUTTONS

In Word pre-2007, click on the Tools menu, choose Macro and a list of Macro options will appear on a sub-menu. These can be used to record and replay macros. In Word 2007–2010, the macro facilities are hidden away on the Developer ribbon tab. This must be displayed before a macro can be created.

Showing the Developer Ribbon Tab

Click on the File menu or Office button and

Above: The Developer ribbon must be displayed in Word 2007–2010 to be able to record a macro.

choose Options or Word Options. From the dialogue box that appears, select Customize Ribbon in the list on the left. Click on the top left drop-down arrow underneath Choose commands from. Select Main Tabs from the list. The list underneath will change to the main ribbon tabs used in Word. Select Developer from this list, then click on the Add button in the middle of the dialogue box. Click on OK to return to the Word screen. The Developer ribbon tab should be displayed along the top of the screen. Click on it to see the buttons that accompany it.

CREATE YOUR OWN MACRO

The following step-by-step guide shows how to record a macro that will create a small table. It will be played by pressing Alt+T on the keyboard.

1. Open Word and a new blank document. In Word 2007–2010, click on the Developer ribbon tab (see the previous section if it's missing) and select the Record Macro button. In earlier versions of Word, click on the Tools menu, select Macro and choose Record New Macro.

2. In all cases, a Record Macro dialogue box will appear. Type a name for your macro (for example, AddTable), then click on the Keyboard button to the right. A second dialogue box will appear. Enter a new keyboard shortcut (in this case, Alt+T) underneath Press new shortcut key. Click on Close and the macro will start to record.

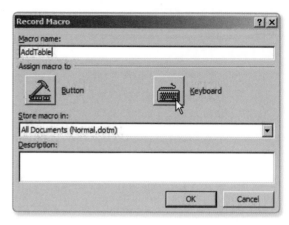

Above: Upon choosing to record a macro, the dialogue box shown here will appear. Enter a meaningful name for the macro and click on Keyboard to assign it a shortcut key.

3. Insert a table (click on the Insert ribbon tab or Table menu) and add some text into the table. Notice that the mouse cannot select the table or any text, but it can operate toolbar buttons, menu options and ribbon tabs. When you have finished recording the macro, click on the Stop Recording button.

> **Hot Tip**
>
> Start recording a macro in Word pre-2007 by double clicking on the letters REC seen at the bottom of the screen.

4. Move down the document and test the macro by pressing the shortcut key allocated for it (Alt+T). The macro should instantly repeat the steps that were recorded.

PLAYING A MACRO

If you can remember the shortcut keys assigned to a macro, then this is one of the quickest methods of playing a macro. However, it's not always easy to remember all the shortcut keys. Instead, press Alt+F8 on the keyboard and a list of macros will appear. Select one from the list and click on the Run button to play it.

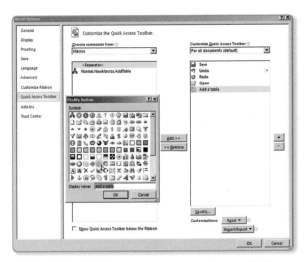

Above: A toolbar button can be added to the Quick Access Toolbar in Word 2007–2010 to run a macro.

Assigning a Macro to the Quick Access Toolbar in Word 2007-2010

Right click on a button on the Quick Access Toolbar and choose Customize Quick Access Toolbar. From the dialogue box that appears, change Popular Commands (listed near the top left underneath Choose commands from:) to Macros. Any macros you've created will be listed on the left. Select your macro and click on Add to transfer it to the Quick Access Toolbar. Select it from here and click on the Modify button to change its icon and display name. Click on OK to close these dialogue boxes and check the macro button is on the Quick Access Toolbar.

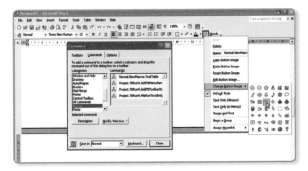

Above: A macro can be assigned to a toolbar button in Word pre-2007.

Assigning a Macro to a Toolbar Button in Word Pre-2007

Right click on any toolbar button and choose Customize. From the dialogue box that appears, select the Commands tab and choose Macros from the list on the left. The list on the right will include the macro you've recorded (it may be called Normal.NewMacros.MacroName). Drag and drop this macro onto a toolbar, then right click on it to change it to a button or text and change or edit the button.

VIEW THE CODE FOR A MACRO

Press Alt+F8 on the keyboard and a Macros dialogue box will appear on the screen. Select a macro from the list and click on the Edit button. Microsoft Visual Basic for Applications will open, revealing the code behind the macro. The code for the macro will begin with the word Sub, followed by the macro's name and two brackets (). Any descriptions are displayed in green (this is not code, just notes) and the macro finishes with the words End Sub.

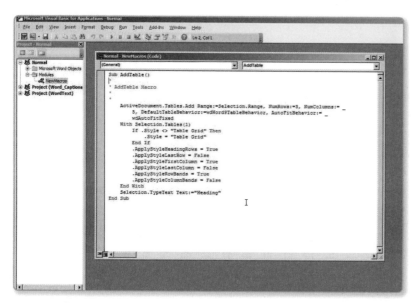

Above: Macros in Word are written in Visual Basic. The code can be viewed and edited.

Edit Macro Code

A macro's Visual Basic code can be changed and new code can be written. If you're new to Visual Basic, try changing a few obvious pieces of code, such as some text that has been created or a font size. If any code is incorrect, the Visual Basic program may alert you at the time of writing, or highlight the error when the macro is run.

Return to Word

When the Microsoft Visual Basic for Applications program is open, Word is also open. To return to Word, click on the X-shaped button in the top-right corner of the Visual Basic program. There is no need to save any changes made to the macro's code as this is done automatically.

CALCULATIONS

Word can produce some simple or sophisticated calculations, which save time on having to open a calculator or spreadsheet and enable numerical information to be included in a document. The following pages show how to create such calculations and include them in a Word document.

QUICK CALCULATIONS

If you need to insert a calculated figure, such as a price including VAT, then there's no need to grab a calculator or open another program – Word can work out the calculation and insert the result into the document. Take a total price, where the price excluding VAT is £100, so the total price including VAT would be calculated as =100×1.2 (in Word it would be written as =100*1.2). The following section shows how to use Word to create such a calculation and insert the result.

Add a Calculation to Word 2007–2010

Click on the Insert ribbon tab, select the Quick Parts button and choose Field. From the dialogue box that appears, make sure (All) is displayed under the Categories section and = (Formula) is selected under the Field names section. Click on the Formula...

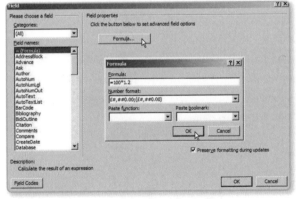

Above: A calculation can be created and the result displayed in a document by creating a formula in Word 2007–2010.

button and a Formula dialogue box will appear. Enter =100*1.2 in the white box at the top (under Formula) and change the Number format by clicking on the drop-down list. Click on OK to return to the first dialogue box and click on OK to see the result displayed in the document.

Hot Tip

A Formula calculation can be changed at a later date by right clicking inside it and choosing Edit Field or Toggle Field Codes.

Add a Calculation to Word Pre-2007

Click on the Table menu and choose Formula (a table doesn't have to be created to do this). A Formula dialogue box will appear on the screen. Enter =100*1.2 in the white box at the top (under Formula) and change the Number format by clicking on the drop-down list. Click on OK to see the result displayed in the document.

CALCULATING TABLE CELLS

A wide range of calculations can be created in a table, allowing values in cells to be averaged, totalled and included in calculations.

Totalling Rows and Columns

If a row or column of cells in a table contains values, Word can calculate a total for them. Select the adjacent cell in the row or column where the total figure will be displayed. Click on the Table menu in Word pre-2007 and choose Formula. In Word 2007–2010, click on the Layout ribbon tab and select the Formula button (it has the letters fx on it). Word may have automatically written the calculation, otherwise write =SUM(ABOVE) or replace ABOVE with BELOW, LEFT or RIGHT to indicate in which direction the values are relative to the selected cell.

Hot Tip

Word can only total a continuous row or column of numbers, so if one cell is empty in a row or column, add a 0 (zero) to it to ensure the total is correctly created.

Calculating an Average in a Row or Column

Word uses a function called Average, which is applied in the same way as totalling a row or column in a table. When the Formula dialogue box is open, replace the SUM function with AVERAGE. For example, if a column of numbers needs to be averaged, select the first empty cell at the bottom of these numbers, open the Formula dialogue box and write =AVERAGE(ABOVE).

Hot Tip

Right click on the Sum formula and choose Update Field to recalculate it.

Find the Highest and Lowest Values in a Row or Column

Create a formula in the same way as adding up a row or column of numbers, but replace the SUM function with MAX to find the highest value or MIN to find the lowest value.

Above: Numbers displayed in a table can be calculated to find totals, averages, highest and lowest values.

Using Cell References to Create Calculations

Every table in Word uses cell references for each cell. The columns are identified by column letters, starting with A, then B and C, and so on. The rows start at number 1 and continue down the table with row 2, 3, 4 and more. Consequently, the top-left cell in a table is referred to as cell A1 and the cell below it is A2. Therefore, creating a formula such as =A1*A2, will multiply the values in cells A1 and A2 (the top-left cell and the one below it).

EQUATIONS IN WORD 2007–2010

Word 2007–2010 includes a set of tools for creating, editing and displaying equations. The equations are regarded as text by Word, so they can be included in a document alongside text. They can be created in Word and transferred to a math-based program. To create an equation in Word, click on the Insert ribbon tab and select the Equation button in the top-right corner of the screen. A list of different types of equations will appear, with options for more equations at the bottom. Once an equation has been created, a new Equation Tools ribbon will appear with a Design tab to allow the equation to be edited.

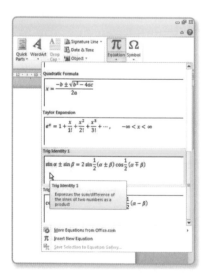

Above: Equations can be created and edited in Word 2007–2010.

USING UP-TO-DATE INFORMATION

Charts, calculations, results and information relating to a document can all be inserted and kept up to date, which is useful if a progress report or the latest sales results need to be reviewed. This section shows how to include information in a document that can be kept up to date.

PASTE LINK FOR DATA AND OBJECTS

Charts and data from programs such as Excel can be copied and pasted into a Word document, but what happens when the chart or data changes in Excel? The pasted information won't be updated unless it is pasted as a link. After copying a chart or some data from another program, don't choose to paste it into the Word document. Instead, click on the Edit menu in Word pre-2007 and choose Paste Special, or click on the Home ribbon tab in Word 2007–2010, select the drop-down arrow below the Paste button and choose Paste Special.

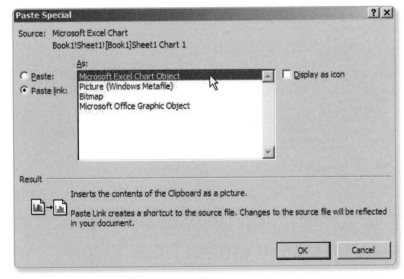

Above: Selecting Paste link allows the pasted object or data to be kept up to date with the original source from which it was copied.

Paste Link from Paste Special

With the Paste Special dialogue box open, select the Paste link option to the left. If this option is not available (greyed-out), then it is not possible to link the copied data or object back to its original source. If it *is* available, select it and choose a type of paste to use, depending on what is being copied (for example, a Microsoft Excel Chart Object, Picture, Bitmap).

Repairing, Updating and Removing a Link in Word 2007-2010

Right click on the linked object or data, select Update Link to check the source file and update the copied item. To repair, remove or change a link, right click on the object or data, select Linked Worksheet Object (or a similar option), then choose Links from the sub-menu. From the dialogue

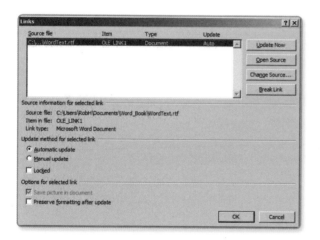

box that appears, any linked data will be listed alongside their source files. Use the buttons on the right side of the dialogue box to update a link, break it, open or change the source file.

Repairing, Updating and Removing a Link in Word Pre-2007

Click on the Edit menu and choose Links. From the dialogue box that appears, any linked data will be listed alongside their source files. Use the buttons on the right side of the dialogue box to update a link, break it, open or change the source file.

Above: Information and objects that have been pasted into a document as links can be controlled via the Links dialogue box.

FIELD INFORMATION

A number of fields can be created in Word to help display up-to-date information concerning a document, including the amount of time spent editing it, when it was last printed and when it was last saved. A field can be inserted into a document by clicking on the Insert menu and choosing Field (Word pre-2007), or clicking on the Insert ribbon tab, selecting Quick Parts and choosing Field from the menu (Word 2007–2010). The following fields can be useful for keeping a track of the progress of a document and can be found under the Date and Time category:

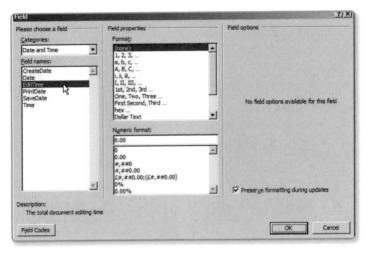

Above: Field codes can be inserted into a document to display information about when the file was created, last printed and how much time has been spent editing it.

→ **CreateDate:** Useful for displaying the date when the document was first created and saved. Reports, dissertations and other long documents can often take weeks, months or years to write, so it's sometimes worthwhile knowing when such a document was started.

→ **EditTime:** The amount of time spent writing the document. Unfortunately, this field doesn't calculate the amount of time spent typing, so if the document is left open on your computer and you don't work on it for a few hours, these will be added to the editing time.

→ **PrintDate:** Printed copies of a document can often become misleading if there is a more up-to-date version, so this field can help to clarify a printed version of a document.

Hot Tip
Right click on a field and choose Update Field to recalculate it and ensure the value it is showing is up to date.

TABS

Tabs are a traditional method of spacing text and displaying it in a uniform style. They are also useful for displaying text on the left and right side of a page. The following pages cover using tabs and typical problems that can arise with them.

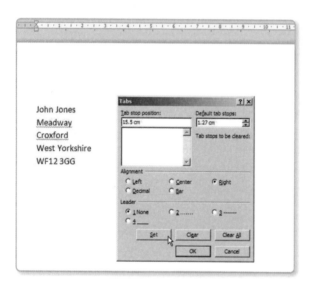

Left: Tabs can be used to display two addresses side by side in a document.

DISPLAY TWO POSTAL ADDRESSES SIDE BY SIDE

A letter should be written with your address near the top right of the page and the recipient's address on the same lines, but on the top left of the page. This can be fiddly to create in Word, but if some tabs are created, then it's much easier. The following step-by-step guide describes how to do this.

1. Write the recipient's address near the top left of the document using left justification. Use several lines for the recipient's address. Once this has been written, select the entire address (move the mouse pointer over the text with the left button held down).

2. Right click inside the selected address text and choose Paragraph from the shortcut menu. A Paragraph dialogue box will appear – click on the Tabs button near the bottom of this box and a smaller Tabs dialogue box will appear.

3. Select the Right option in the Tabs dialogue box, then enter a value in the top box, underneath Tab stop position. This represents the far right edge where your own address will be written. On an A4 page, enter 15.5 cm. Click on the Set button to add this tab, then click on OK to return to the document.

4. A right tab has now been created for the lines in the document where the recipient's address is displayed. Position the cursor at the end of the text on the first line of the recipient's address. Press the Tab key once on the keyboard. The cursor should now be on the right-hand side of the page. Type the first line of your address.

5. Continue typing your address by positioning the cursor at the end of the text for the recipient's address, then press the Tab key once on the keyboard to move to the right side of the page.

Hot Tip

The ruler shows tab markings and their justification. An 'L' shape indicates a left-justified tab marking, but if the L is the wrong way round, it is right-justified.

USING TABS FOR COLUMNS OF TEXT

Whilst a table is often easier to create and display text in columns, tabs are the traditional method and it is worthwhile knowing how to use them.

Setting Up Tabs

Tabs can be created before or after text has been written, but it's often easier to set them up before the text is added to a document. If the document contains no text that needs to be tabbed, right click inside it and choose Paragraph. If the document contains text that needs to be tabbed, select it and right click inside the selected text, then choose Paragraph. From the dialogue box that appears, click on the Tabs button and a Tabs dialogue box will appear. Use this dialogue box to set all the required tabs. The following list explains the different alignment options for tabs:

Left: Text is left justified to the tab marker.
Right: Text is right justified to the tab marker.
Center: Text is centred to the tab marker.
Decimal: If a decimal point is included in a number, the text will be justified to it.
Bar: A vertical line is added to each line.

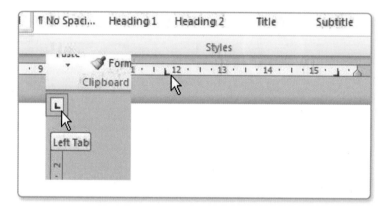

Setting Tabs on the Ruler

Make sure the ruler is displayed along the top of the page. If it's not, first check you are in Print Layout or Normal/Draft view. Next, click on the View menu or ribbon tab and select Ruler from the menu or tick

Above: Tabs can be set on the ruler by selecting a type of tab from the tab marker in the top-left corner of the page and then clicking on the ruler to add them.

box. In the top-left corner of the page, there should be an L-shaped button, just below the ribbon or toolbars. This indicates a left-aligned tab, but click on it and various other tabs can be chosen. Click on a part of the horizontal ruler and a tab will be set.

Tabs Trouble

Tabs can make a mess of a page and in some cases they need to be removed. They can be dragged off the ruler, or removed by returning to the Tabs dialogue box and selecting the Clear All button. Tabs will only be removed from selected lines of text, so if you want to remove all the tabs from a section of text, select it first.

Above: A tabulated column of text can be selected with the mouse by holding down the Alt key at the same time.

Copying and Deleting Tabbed Text

If some text has been tabbed so that it is displayed in columns, a column of text can be copied or deleted. Hold down the Alt key on the keyboard and move the mouse pointer over a column of text with the left button held down. By holding down the Alt key, only the text the mouse pointer moves over is selected. You can then choose to cut, copy or delete the selected text.

CREATE AN INDEX

Word can locate and mark keywords throughout a document, then create an index which refers to them and their relevant page numbers. The following section shows how to set this up and create an index at the end of a document.

Mark Index Entry

Index

Main entry: | Paste Link

Subentry: |

Options

○ Cross-reference: | See

● Current page

○ Page range

Bookmark: |

Page number format

☐ Bold

☐ Italic

This dialog box stays open so that you can mark multiple index entries.

| Mark | Mark All | Cancel |

Above: Keywords need to be marked in a document before creating an index.

MARK THE ENTRIES

An index uses keywords called marked index entries to refer to words in a book and indicate the page numbers where they can be found. This can be done quickly, even if the document is very long. Move to the start of the document and select a word to be included in the index. Press Alt+Shift+X on the keyboard and a Mark Index Entry dialogue box will appear. The selected word will appear at the top of the dialogue box, next to Main entry. Make sure Current page is selected, then click on the Mark All button. Word will check through the document for every instance where this word appears and include it in the index. Alternatively, click on the Mark button and Word will only include this instance in the index.

Continue Marking

Move down the document and select another word to include in the index. Click back inside the Mark Index Entry dialogue box and select the Mark button or the Mark All button. Once all relevant text has been marked for the index, close the Mark Index Entry dialogue box. Some code will appear next to each marked text, but this isn't visible when printed – it can be hidden

by clicking on the Show/Hide button on the Home ribbon tab or Standard toolbar. You can return to the Mark Index Entry dialogue box and mark more entries, even after the index has been created.

INSERT THE INDEX

Move to the end of the document (press Ctrl+End), then click on the References ribbon tab in Word 2007–2010 and select the Insert Index button or in Word pre-2007, click on the Insert menu and choose Index and Tables, or Reference followed by Index and Tables from the sub-menu. In all cases, a dialogue box will appear. Make sure the Index tab is selected in the dialogue box, then choose some settings for the index (number of columns, Right align page numbers). Click on OK to close the dialogue box and insert the index into the document.

Update the Index

If the index needs updating because page numbers have changed or new and existing marked entries have been added, right click inside it and choose Update Field. If new words need to be added to the index, mark these entries, then update the index and they will be automatically added.

Right: An index can use a variety of designs and styles.

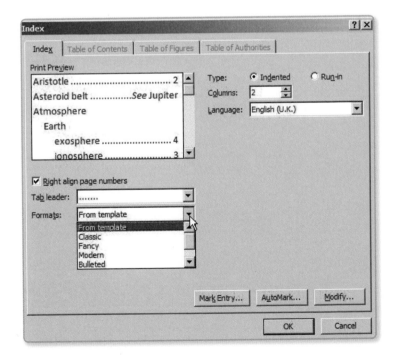

USING REFERENCES FOR QUOTES AND SOURCES

If a document contains quotes and information from other sources, this can be referenced using Word's endnotes and footnotes, or by creating a table of authorities. Similarly, tables, figures and equations included in a document can be listed to display their locations.

TYPES OF REFERENCING

There are several approaches to referencing quotes and other information in a document. These vary according to academic styles and preferences by academic and other institutions. However, there are a number of referencing techniques used by Word, which can help to organize references and their sources. These include the following:

➔ **Endnotes and footnotes:** These are useful for referencing quotes and providing further relevant information.

➔ **Table of authorities:** Used with legal documents where cases, statutes and regulations are quoted.

➔ **Table of figures:** Creates a list of all the tables, figures and equations used in a document. It can be used to create a contents page of diagrams.

ENDNOTES AND FOOTNOTES

One of the easiest methods of referencing quotes and other information is to add either a footnote at the bottom of the page or an endnote at the end of the document. Word can automatically number each footnote or endnote and allocate space to write the required source information.

Insert an Endnote or Footnote in Word 2007-2010

Position the cursor at the end of the text which needs to be referenced. Click on the References ribbon tab, then select Insert Footnote or Insert Endnote. A number will appear next to the text where the cursor was last positioned and Word will move to the bottom of the page for a Footnote or

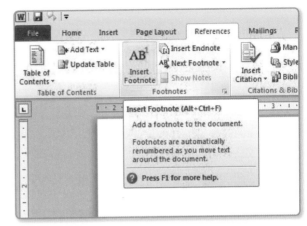

Above: Footnotes and endnotes in Word 2007–2010 can be found on the References ribbon tab.

the end of the document for an Endnote. The same number will be inserted at the bottom of the page or document, allowing you to type a reference or note.

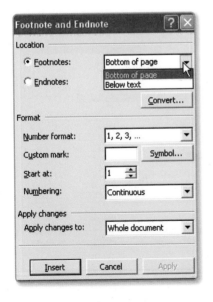

Left: Word pre-2007 uses a separate dialogue box to enter footnotes and endnotes.

Insert an Endnote or Footnote in Word Pre-2007

Position the cursor at the end of the text which needs to be referenced. Click on the Insert menu and choose Footnote, or Reference followed by Footnote from the sub-menu. A Footnote and Endnote dialogue box will appear. Select either Footnote or Endnote and choose where to display the reference or note. Select a numbering format and click on the Insert or OK button. A number will appear

Hot Tip

Press Alt+Ctrl+F to insert a footnote.

Hot Tip

Press Ctrl+Alt+D to insert an endnote.

next to the text where the cursor was last positioned and Word will move to the footnote or endnote and display the same number. Type some text for the footnote or endnote.

Viewing Endnotes and Footnotes in the Text

When you spot a number in the text that represents a footnote or endnote, position the mouse pointer over it and a small comment box will appear. Keep the mouse pointer over the number and the footnote or endnote will appear on the screen.

Editing a Footnote or Endnote

Footnotes and endnotes can be edited in the same way as normal text. Just click inside the text at the bottom of the page or end of the document and change it.

Hot Tip

Double click on the footnote or endnote number in a document and Word will jump to the text for it, and vice versa.

Deleting a Footnote or Endnote

If a number representing a footnote or endnote is deleted in the text, the corresponding reference at the bottom of the page or end of the document will also be deleted.

TABLE OF AUTHORITIES

A table of authorities is often used in legal documents where cases, laws and regulations need to be referenced.

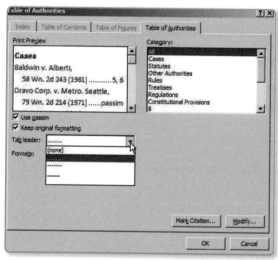

Above: A table of authorities is used in legal documents to refer to cases, laws and statutes.

The table of authorities is similar to an index or table of contents, but uses citations to refer to specific lines of text and can group them into different categories (cases, statutes, rules). The first step in creating a table of authorities is to mark the citations.

Mark the Citations

Locate a piece of text that needs to be marked as a citation, then click on the References ribbon tab in Word 2007–2010 and choose the Mark Citation button, or click on the Insert menu in Word pre-2007 and then select

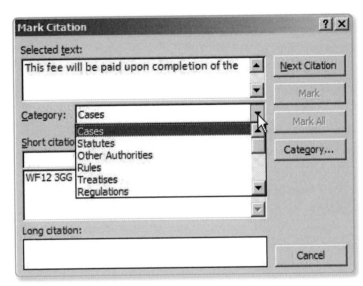

Above: Citations are added to text in a document and grouped according to different categories. They can then be included in a table of authorities.

Index and Tables, or Reference followed by Index and Tables from the sub-menu. Select the Table of Authorities tab inside the dialogue box that appears and click on the Mark Citation button near the bottom. With the Mark Citation dialogue box on screen, complete the details for the citation, then click on the Mark button. The dialogue box can remain on screen whilst more citations are added.

Create a Table of Authorities

After marking a number of citations, select a point in the document to display the table of authorities, then click on the References ribbon tab in Word 2007–2010 and select the Insert Table of Authorities button. In Word pre-2007, click on the Insert menu and then choose Index

Hot Tip

Open the Mark Citation dialogue box by pressing Shift+Alt+I on the keyboard.

Hot Tip

Update a table of authorities by right clicking on it and choosing Update Field.

and Tables, or Reference followed by Index and Tables. In both cases, a dialogue box will appear – make sure the Table of Authorities tab is selected. Choose any options for the style of the table, then click on OK.

TABLE OF FIGURES FOR DIAGRAMS AND TABLES

A table of figures is similar to a contents page, but all the entries refer to illustrations and tables with captions.

Hot Tip

Update a table of figures by right clicking on it and choosing Update Field.

Create Captions

The first step in creating a table of figures is to add captions to any tables and images in a document. Right click on the image, object or table and choose Caption. Alternatively, select the image, table or object, then click on the Insert menu in Word pre-2007 and choose Caption, or Reference followed by Caption from the sub-menu. In Word 2007–2010, click on the References ribbon tab and select the Insert Caption button. In all cases a dialogue box will appear with some options for captioning. Click on OK and the caption will appear next to the image, object or table.

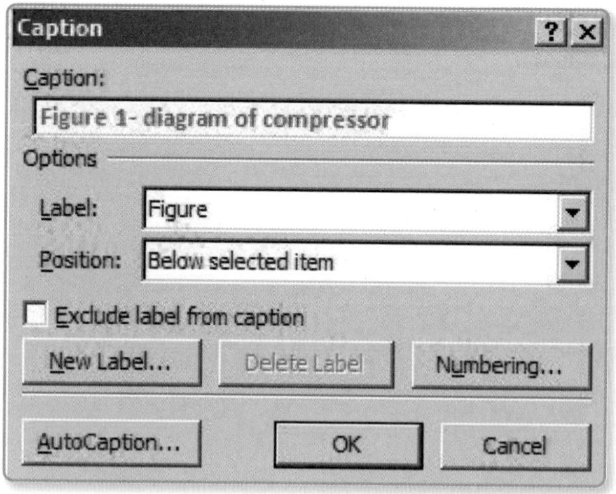

Left: Captions can accompany tables, objects and images and can be used in the creation of a table of figures.

Create a Table of Figures

Once several captions have been added, position the cursor at a point in the document where the table of figures will be displayed. In Word 2007–2010, click on the References ribbon tab and select the Insert Table of Figures button. In earlier versions of Word, click on the Insert menu and choose Index and Tables, or Reference followed by Index and Tables (select the Table of Figures tab). In all cases, choose a style for the table of figures, then click on OK. A table of figures will be inserted into the document.

Hot Tip

Jump to an object, image or table listed in a table of figures by holding down the Ctrl key and left clicking on it.

DOCUMENT SECURITY

Word documents often need to have some level of security to ensure they are not edited by the wrong people and not copied and used elsewhere. There are a number of security methods available in Word, which are outlined in the following section.

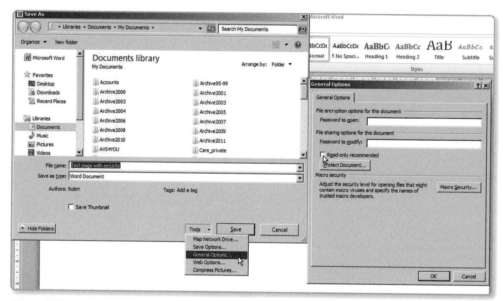

Above: A Word document can be saved with a password for opening it and a separate password for modifying it.

SAVE WITH A PASSWORD

A Word document can be saved with a password for opening and anoher for modifying the document. Open the Save As dialogue box (press F12 on the keyboard). Click on the Tools menu button inside it and from the short menu that appears, select General Options or Security Options. A second dialogue box will appear with some options for entering a password to open the document and another password to modify it. There is also a tick box for Read-only recommended, which will not allow anyone else to modify the document unless they save it with a different name.

DOCUMENT PROTECTION IN WORD PRE-2007

A document can be protected in a number of ways in Word pre-2007. Click on the Tools menu and choose Protect Document. From the dialogue box that appears, select one of the following and enter an optional password:

⊖ **Tracked changes:** Any amendments will be displayed as tracked changes (see chapter four for further details).

⊖ **Comments:** Text can be copied, but not cut or deleted. New text cannot be added to the document.

⊖ **Forms:** Text can only be typed where form tools (combo boxes, drop-down lists, text boxes) have been inserted. Text cannot be selected, so it cannot be copied or deleted.

DOCUMENT PROTECTION IN WORD 2007-2010

Click on the Review ribbon tab and select the Restrict Editing button near the top-right corner of the screen. A Restrict Formatting and Editing pane will be displayed down the right-hand side of the screen. There are three steps to using this pane. The first provides formatting restrictions, the second concerns editing and the last switches on the editing restrictions with an optional password.

Formatting Restrictions

Select the tick box labelled Limit formatting to a selection of styles, then click on Settings below. A Formatting Restrictions dialogue box will open, allowing particular fonts to be

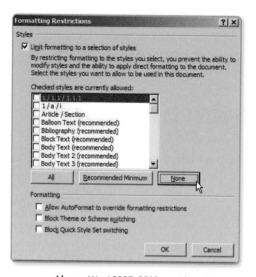

Above: Word 2007–2010 provides editing restrictions, which include specifying the fonts that can and cannot be used in a document.

selected. This is useful for a document where other people edit it and use the wrong font.

Editing Restrictions

Add a tick mark to the box labelled Allow only this type of editing in the document. A drop-down list will appear underneath with options for tracked changes, comments, filling in forms and no changes (read only). These are the same options that are included in Word pre-2007 and are explained earlier in this section.

Exceptions (Optional)

Specific people can be selected to be able to edit the document freely. This feature is available where Word can communicate with a computer network and select users.

PORTABLE DOCUMENT FORMAT (PDF)

The Portable Document Format (PDF) is a popular type of file that can be shared around the world and opened by most computers using Adobe Reader software, which is free to use. The advantage of a PDF is that unless you have PDF editing software, the file can only be read and cannot be edited. Microsoft Word 2007 and later versions can save a document as a PDF and this is covered in greater detail in chapter five.

WATERMARKS FOR PRINTED DOCUMENTS

A watermark is a faint piece of text or an image that is displayed across each page and is useful for ensuring a printed document is not photocopied or displaying the author of a manuscript. Further information on inserting a watermark into a Word document is covered in chapter three.

SPEECH RECOGNITION, DICTATION AND NARRATION

Text can be read by the computer or you can dictate text into Word using software and tools that are freely available with Word and Windows. The following section shows how to set up voice recognition and narration, and outlines some of the problems that can arise.

Left: Windows Vista and Windows 7 have some useful tools, including a narrator and speech-recognition software. These can be opened via the Start menu.

SPEECH RECOGNITION IN WORD 2007–2010

Windows Vista and Windows 7 include speech recognition and narration software, so they are not included with Word 2007 or 2010. To access these tools, click on the Start menu, select All Programs, choose Ease of Access and select Windows Speech Recognition. If this program has not been used before, you will need to set up speech recognition. A series of dialogue boxes will appear, enabling the software to set up the microphone and start understanding the way you speak. This software can also examine the documents you write and try to understand any common words and phrases used.

Hot Tip

When setting up speech recognition, see the reference sheet for all the commands that can be spoken when dictating text into Word.

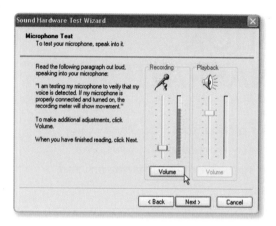

Left: If your microphone cannot pick up any sounds, Windows has a number of settings and test procedures to help.

Microphone Trouble

If your microphone seems to be switched off, but it is definitely connected, open the Control Panel via the Start menu, select the icon or option concerning sound or audio and look for a section concerning the microphone. Depending on the version of Windows, there may be an option to test the hardware or playback the microphone through the speakers.

NARRATION IN WORD 2007-2010

Windows Vista and Windows 7 use their own narration software to read whatever is on the screen. Click on the Start menu, select All Programs, choose Ease of Access and select Narrator. The Narrator can be set to read the contents of whatever is on the screen. There are a number of options concerning the speed of reading and the style. These can be found within the Narrator program.

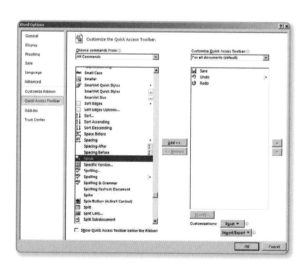

Narrator Doesn't Work in Word 2007-2010

If Windows Narrator does not read back any text in a Word document, then a Speak button needs to be added to the Quick Access Toolbar to enable the program to read back text. Right click on any button on

Above: Adding a Speak button to the Quick Access Toolbar enables text to be read aloud.

Hot Tip

Press the Ctrl key on the keyboard to stop the Narrator reading aloud.

the Quick Access Toolbar and choose Customize Quick Access Toolbar. From the dialogue box that appears, click on the drop-down list in the top-left corner (under Choose commands from:) and select All Commands. Scroll down the long list on the left and select Speak. Click on the Add button to transfer it to the list on the right, then click on OK.

Read It back via the Speak Button

A new button has now been added to the Quick Access Toolbar. Now you can select some text in Word and click on it to have the text read aloud. If you find Narrator is reading something else, press Ctrl to stop this, then select the text in the document and click on the Speak button. The selected text will then be read out by Narrator. The Narrator program now does not need to be open to have text read out aloud.

SPEECH RECOGNITION AND NARRATION IN WORD PRE-2007

Click on the Tools menu and choose Speech. If the speech recognition and narration tools have not been used before, they may need to be installed (the Word or Office CD may be required). Word's voice recognition can be set up to learn your voice. A series of dialogue boxes will appear, allowing the microphone to be set up and several sentences to be read aloud to establish your pronunciation.

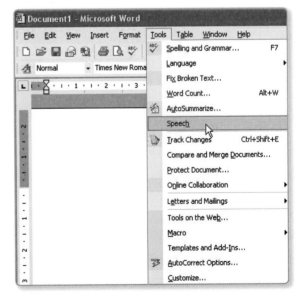

Right: Word pre-2007 has speech recognition and narration tools included. These are accessed via the Tools menu.

The Language Bar

All of the speech tools available with Word pre-2007 are displayed along the Language Bar, which is usually positioned across the top of the screen. This bar can be customized to display text buttons or icon buttons for dictation, reading text (Speak Text) and voice commands (menu options).

Language Bar Speech Tools

Click on the Speech Tools button on the Language Bar in Word pre-2007 and choose Options. From the dialogue box that appears there are a number of options for customizing how the speech tools work. For example, click on the Settings button to allocate keyboard keys for switching between dictating text and using voice commands to operate menus and open programs.

Above: The dictation and speech may need to be customized to make it work correctly. This can be done using options accessed via the Language Bar in Word pre-2007.

Spoken Text in Word Pre-2007

Select the text in Word that you want read aloud, then click on the Speak Text button on the Language Bar. Word will read this text aloud. Make sure your speakers are switched on to be able to hear the text being read.

TROUBLESHOOTING SPEECH RECOGNITION AND NARRATION

Setting up speech recognition can be very frustrating because the software needs to learn how you speak and there are numerous settings that need tweaking to make this tool more effective. You'll need several hours perfecting speech recognition and if you encounter difficulties, use the help facilities and search for answers to problems using the Internet.

PRINTING ON TO ENVELOPES AND LABELS

Word can be used to print addresses and other text on to envelopes and labels to help produce professional-looking stationery. The following section provides step-by-step information on how to do this in the various versions of the program.

PRINTING ON TO AN ENVELOPE

Click on the Mailings ribbon tab in Word 2007–2010 and select the Envelopes button in the top-left corner of the screen, or click on the Tools menu in earlier versions of Word and select Envelopes and Labels, or click on Letters and Mailings, then select Envelopes and Labels. In all cases, an Envelopes and Labels dialogue box will appear on the screen. Type a delivery address to print on to the envelope and, if required, type a return address (sender's address).

Change the Envelope Size

Click on the Options button to check the size of the envelope is correct. If it's wrong, click on a drop-down list underneath Envelope size to choose a different size of envelope. If the size of your envelope is not listed, choose Custom size at the bottom of the list and a small box will appear allowing you to enter the width and height of the envelope.

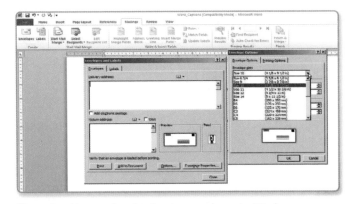

Above: An address can be printed on to an envelope using Word. The size of the envelope can be set and both the delivery address and sender's address can be printed.

Change the Font and Position of the Address

From within the Envelope Options dialogue box (click on the Options button in the Envelope and Labels dialogue box), the type of font used for the delivery and return addresses can be changed and the position of the text can be adjusted.

PRINTING LABELS

Word can create a sheet of labels with the same text on each label, or print text on to one label. Click on the Mailings ribbon tab in Word 2007–2010 and select the Labels button in the top-left corner of the screen, or click on the Tools menu in earlier versions of Word and select Envelopes and Labels, or click on Letters and Mailings, then select Envelopes and Labels. In all cases, an Envelopes and Labels dialogue box will appear on the screen. Select the Labels tab and enter an address or other text to appear on each label. Choose either a full page of the same label, or a single label.

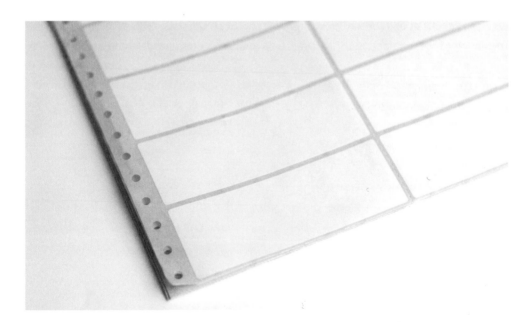

Change the Size of the Labels

Click on the Options button inside the Envelopes and Labels dialogue box and a second dialogue box will appear with a list of different labels. Choose a label product (Avery, Microsoft, Tico) and a particular label product number (usually found on your box of labels). If your labels are not listed, select the New Labels button and set the dimensions of the labels.

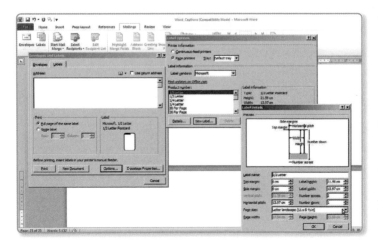

Above: Word can print on to labels. A variety of different label dimensions are stored, but you can also create your own labels and specify the dimensions.

Creating a Labels Document

If you want to save a sheet of labels and print them again in the future, then Word can create a document. After selecting the type of label and entering the text to appear on each label or one label, click on the New Document button inside the Envelopes and Labels dialogue box. The dialogue box will close and the labels will appear in a document in Word. This can now be saved, printed and printed again in the future.

Typical Label Printing Problems

One of the most common problems when printing labels is the text not being aligned with each label, so it is usually printed across two labels. A ruler can help here to check the exact dimensions of the sheet of labels with the dimensions set up in Word. Return to the Envelopes and Labels dialogue box and the Labels tab, click on the Options button and the Label Options dialogue box will open. Click on the Details button and a third dialogue box will appear, displaying all the dimensions for each label and the gaps between them. This may help to resolve the problem outlined here.

EDITING IMAGES

Most images inserted into a Word document can be edited to allow text to flow around or over them. Also, the brightness, contrast and colours used in images such as a logo, can be changed in Word to help improve its presentation.

ALIGNING TEXT WITH AN IMAGE

When an image is inserted into a document (for example, a photo, logo, diagram, chart), some accompanying text may need to be displayed alongside it. Right click inside the image and in Word 2007–2010, select Wrap Text and choose one of the options from the sub-menu that

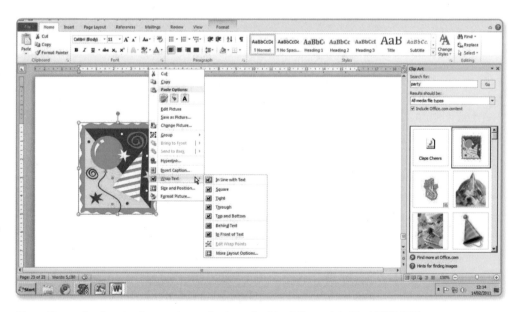

Above: Text can be aligned and wrapped around an image by right clicking on it in Word 2007–2010.

Hot Tip

Drag and drop an image to different positions inside a document and Word will wrap the text around it according to the settings you've selected.

appears. In earlier versions of Word, right click on the image and choose Format Picture or Format Object. From the dialogue box that appears, select the Layout tab and choose a wrapping style for the text.

ADJUSTING AN IMAGE

The brightness and contrast applied to most images (drawings and photographs) can be adjusted in Word, along with converting them to black and white or grayscale and cropping their size. These tools are available on the Picture toolbar in Word pre-2007 and on the Picture Tools Format ribbon tab in Word 2007–2010.

Hot Tip

If the Picture toolbar doesn't appear on the screen after selecting an image in Word pre-2007, right click on any toolbar button and choose Picture from the shortcut menu that appears.

Adjusting Brightness and Contrast

Select an image to adjust its brightness and contrast. Depending on the version of Word, the following instructions should be followed:

- **Photographs in Word 2007–2010**: Right click inside the image and choose Format Picture. From the dialogue box that appears, select Picture Corrections from the list on the left, then drag the sliders for the brightness and contrast. The picture will be instantly adjusted.

- **Images in Word 2007–2010**: Select the image and make sure the Picture Tools Format ribbon tab is selected. Use the Brightness and Contrast buttons in the top-right corner of the screen to adjust the image.

➲ **Word pre-2007**: Select the image and the Picture toolbar button will appear on screen. Click on the More Contrast and Less Contrast buttons on the toolbar. There are also two brightness (more and less brightness) buttons.

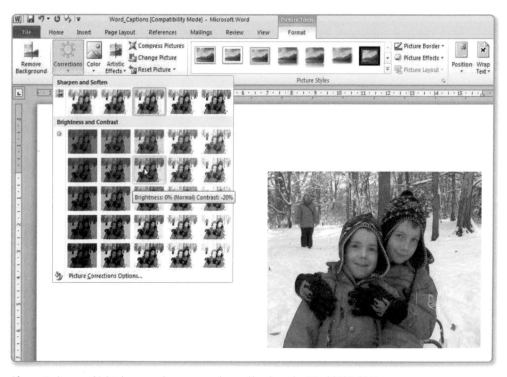

Above: A photograph's brightness and contrast can be quickly adjusted in Word 2007–2010 using the Corrections ribbon button.

Sharpen and Soften a Photograph in Word 2007–2010

Select the photograph and the Picture Tools Format ribbon tab should be selected with a number of ribbon buttons across the top of the screen. Click on the Corrections button and a palette of corrected images will appear to help soften, sharpen and adjust the brightness of the image.

Convert to Black and White

Select the image and, in Word 2007–2010, make sure the Picture Tools Format ribbon tab is selected, then click on the Color or Recolor button. From the palette of options or menu that appears, select Grayscale under the Recolor section. In Word pre-2007, select the image and click on the Color button that's second from the left on the Picture toolbar. A short menu will drop down: choose Grayscale (do not select Black & White) from this menu and the image will be converted. In all versions of Word, the image can be changed back to colour by returning to the appropriate menu (choose Automatic in Word pre-2007).

CROPPING AN IMAGE

If only part of an image needs to be included in a document, or it needs trimming to remove any unwanted space around the edges, then it can be cropped. This is not the same as resizing an image and only trims it.

> ## Hot Tip
>
> In Word 2007–2010, different ribbon buttons appear between editing a photograph and a Clip Art image.

Cropping an Image in Word 2007-2010

Select the image and make sure the Picture Tools Format ribbon is displayed along the top of the screen. Click on the drop-down arrow underneath the Crop button and a number of cropping options will appear. Crop to shape, for example, allows the image to be changed to a shape, such as a round box or circle. Aspect ratio provides a list of pre-set ratios for width and height (most photographs use an aspect ratio of 3:2). The Crop option allows manual cropping.

Manual Cropping in Word 2007-2010

After selecting an image and choosing the Crop button on the Picture Tools Format ribbon button (or the Crop menu option), position the mouse over the crop markers at the corner or edges of the image. When the mouse pointer changes to a 't' shape or 'L' shape, hold the left button down to move into the image and crop a corner or edge. Release the left button to stop cropping.

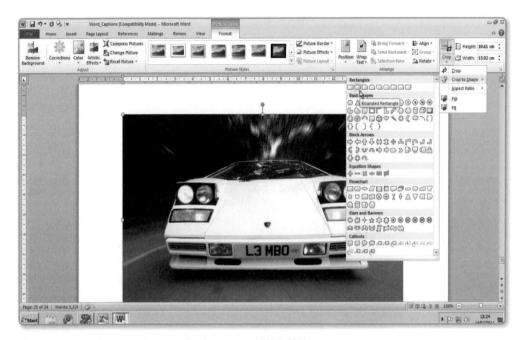

Above: Images can be cropped to a specific shape in Word 2007–2010.

Cropping an Image in Word Pre-2007

Select the image and make sure the Picture toolbar is displayed on screen. Click on the Crop button in the middle of the toolbar and the mouse pointer will adopt the crop image. Position the mouse pointer over any of the dots on the corners or edges of the image. Hold the left button down and the mouse pointer will change to a 't' shape or 'L' shape. Move the mouse pointer into the image to crop it, then release the left button to stop cropping.

CHANGING COLOURS IN AN IMAGE

The individual colours used in some images can be changed in Word. This doesn't usually apply to photographs because the images and colours used are too complex, but it can be used for logos and general Clip Art.

Ungroup the Image

The first stage in changing the colours used in an image is to ungroup it so that individual colours can be selected and altered. Right click on the image, choose Edit Picture or, if this is not available, select Grouping, followed by Ungroup from the sub-menu. In some cases, a dialogue box will appear warning that the image will need to be converted to be able to edit it.

Select a Colour to Change

Once the image has been ungrouped or the Edit Picture option chosen, try left clicking on part of the image and a small section of it will be selected (a series of dots or squares will appear around the selected part of the image). Double click inside

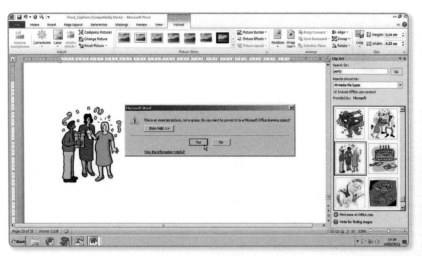

Above: Ungrouping an image helps to change individual colours within it. A warning message may appear when doing this.

this selected part of the image and either a dialogue box will appear (click on the Colors and Lines tab) or a ribbon tab will appear across the top of the screen. Choose a different colour from the ribbon tab or dialogue box and the colour used in the selected part of the image will be changed.

Delete Part of an Image

The same method for selecting part of an image and changing its colour can also be used for deleting part of an image. Once a part has been selected, press Delete on the keyboard and it will be removed from the image.

FURTHER READING

How to Write Your Own Effective Employee Handbook in 1 Hour or Less: With Microsoft Word-Compatible Template on Companion CD-ROM, Atlantic Publishing Group Inc, 2011.

Microsoft Office Word 2007 (Microsoft Official Academic Course for exam 77-601), John Wiley & Sons, 2008.

Microsoft Word 2003 Expert Skills (Microsoft Official Academic Course), John Wiley & Sons, 2004.

Bryan, Laura, *Microsoft Word for Healthcare Documentation: A Guide for Transcriptionists, Editors, and Health Information Professionals*, Lippincott Williams & Wilkins, 2010.

Cram, Carol M. and Duffy, Jennifer, *Microsoft Office Word 14: Medical Professionals*, South-Western, Division of Thomson Learning, 2011.

Duffy, Jennifer, *Microsoft Office Word 2010 Advanced: Illustrated Course Guide*, South-Western College Publishing, 2011.

Foy, Geoffrey, *Text Production with Microsoft Word 2007*, Gill & Macmillan Ltd, 2009.

Holden, Paul and Munnelly, Brendan, *ECDL Advanced Word Processing for Microsoft Office XP and Office 2003*, Prentice Hall, 2006.

Lambert, Joan and Cox, Joyce, *MOS 2010 Study Guide for Microsoft Word, Excel, PowerPoint and Outlook*, Microsoft Press, 2011.

Marshall, James J., *Beginning Microsoft Word Business Documents: From Novice to Professional*, APRESS, 2006.

Matthews, Marty, *Microsoft Office Word 2007 QuickSteps (How to Do Everything)*, McGraw-Hill Osborne, 2007.

Munnelly, Brendan, *ECDL4: The Complete Coursebook for Microsoft Office XP*, Prentice Hall, 2003.

O'Leary, Linda I., *Microsoft Word 2010: A Case Approach, Complete*, McGraw-Hill Higher Education, 2011.

Rourke, Claire, *Advanced Training for ECDL – Word Processing: The Complete Course for Advanced Word Processing in Microsoft Word in Windows XP and Office 2007*, Blackrock Education Centre, 2010.

Schorr, Ben, *The Lawyer's Guide to Microsoft Word 2007*, American Bar Association, 2010.

Shelly, Gary B.; Cashman, Thomas J.; and Vermaat, Misty E., *Microsoft Word 2002: Comprehensive Concepts and Techniques (Shelly Cashman Series)*, Course Technology Inc, 2001.

Shepard, Aaron, *Perfect Pages: Self Publishing with Microsoft Word, or How to Design Your Own Book for Desktop Publishing and Print on Demand (Word 97–2003 for Windows, Word 2004 for Mac)*, Shepard Publications, 2006.

Tommy, A., *Microsoft Office Specialist Word 2003 Core Book/CD Package: Core Exam Preparation Guide*, ENI Publishing, 2004.

Tyson, Herb, *Teach Yourself Web Publishing with Microsoft Word in a Week*, Pearson Education Ltd, 1995.

Wempen, Faithe, *Microsoft Word 2010 in Depth*, QUE, 2010

WEBSITES

http://daiya.mvps.org/bookwordframes.htm
How to write a book using Microsoft Word.

http://msdn.microsoft.com/en-us/library/ff604039.aspx
If you've read the section in this book covering macros and want to look further into the subject, then this official website is the next stage.

www.baycongroup.com/wlesson0.htm
Free online tutorials for Microsoft Word 2007.

www.btinternet.com/~uyea/docs/word_dissertation-1.html
Guidance on writing a dissertation using Microsoft Word.

www.microsoft.com/education/howto.mspx
How-to articles from Microsoft, covering everything from adding borders and drawings to creating a calendar and using international characters.

www.microsoft.com/learning
Microsoft-certified online courses to learn valuable skills on various Microsoft products.

www.msofficeforums.com/word
Forum covering all Microsoft Office software, including a section for Word.

www.office.microsoft.com/en-us/word-help
Microsoft's official website for help and trouble-shooting involving past and current versions of Word.

www.officefrustration.com
Useful Microsoft Office-related forum with lots of discussions concerning Word.

www.wordbanter.com
A forum that focus on Word and Word-related topics.

INDEX